STRAT
SOC

*The Challenge of Labour's
Programme*

Stuart Holland

SPOKESMAN BOOKS
1975

DEDICATION

To those in the Labour movement who are fighting for the socialist strategy of the 1974 manifestos, and against the psuedo-manifestists who fear to challenge capitalism.

Published by the Bertrand Russell Peace Foundation Ltd., Bertrand Russell House, Gamble Street, Nottingham NG7 4ET for *Spokesman Books*.

© Spokesman Books 1975

Printed by the Russell Press Limited, Gamble Street, Nottingham NG7 4ET. (Tel: 0602 - 74505).

Contents

	Preface	4
	Introduction	5
1.	Class and Inequality	7
2.	The State and Economic Power	13
3.	The Trend to Monopoly	17
4.	The Multinational Dimension	26
5.	Public Money in the Private Sector	33
6.	The Unmixed Economy	38
7.	Public Ownership of Leading Firms	43
8.	Countervailing Multinationals	49
9.	Size and Selection	56
10.	The Planning Agreements System	62
11.	Planning and Industrial Democracy	69
12.	Socialism and the Social Contract	77
	References	83
	Figures	89

Preface

This work is substantially derived from my book *The Socialist Challenge,* to be published shortly by Quartet Books.

Because *The Socialist Challenge* has proved to be a major work (at least in terms of length) there seemed a strong case for publishing a short version in this form. Naturally I hope that any interest (or criticism) provoked by this version will encourage readers to delve in the longer work.

I am grateful to Quartet Books for permission to publish some of the material from *The Socialist Challenge* in this book, as well as to Spokesman Books for publishing it.

The text was completed before the February 1974 general election, and only edited thereafter, with an up-dating of references, including government publications such as the August 1974 White Paper, *The Regeneration of British Industry* and the January 1975 Industry Bill.

Stuart Holland
February 1975

Note

Meso-economics in this text basically means monopoly capital or big league private enterprise *between* conventional macro and micro economics.

Introduction

In the early 1970's the Labour Party shaped a radical new strategy for socialism. This programme, published by the Party in 1973, was based on a re-distribution of wealth, a major extension of public ownership, new public accountability and controls over big business, and a radical extension of industrial democracy.

Much of the radicalism of this Programme is still only sensed rather than understood by many people round the country. They know that something is wrong with the British economy and that in the mess which Labour inherited from the Tories in the spring of 1974 working people suffer more than the middle and upper classes. On the other hand, many people do not see the link between the crisis in the economy and changes in the recent structure of British capitalism. They identify the new public ownership proposals with old style nationalisation, despite the fact that they are crucially different. They do not grasp the fact that big private enterprise now dominates the heart of the industrial economy, and that its failure to generate investment, jobs, and exports or sell goods at reasonable prices underlies the problems of high unemployment, depreciated take-home pay, a national economy in debt abroad and soaring inflation in the shops.

This short work sets out the kind of reasons why the Labour Party shaped its new radical strategy for a fundamental shift in the present imbalance between public and private power. It shows both the massive job which must be done, started by a majority Labour government, and the fact that only Labour's socialist policies can hope to transform the problems we are faced with now.

CHAPTER ONE

Class and Inequality

There are some calls today for moderate economic policies. Some of these are forwarded with claims that the language of class politics is outdated and that the Party's proposals for new public ownership should be softened down if it is to win the floating voter and the 'middle ground' of politics.

In political terms, by definition, the 'middle ground' should represent those voters placed mid- or half-way in the voting population. But this middle ground should not be confused with the middle class, which is *far above* the middle of the range of incomes in the working population. Centrism which amounts to maintaining middle and upper class dominance in society is not so much moderation as an immoderate support for a minority versus the majority of the people.

Working class people sense class differences well enough in terms of the 'them-versus-us' feeling. But Michael Barratt Brown has shown that this feeling is proved a fact in terms of the minority distribution of professional and supervisory jobs. As illustrated in figure 1, Britain is divided between a small upper class of professional and capital owning people (the top ten per cent); an equally small professional and supervisory class (the next ten per cent), and a working class constituting the remaining four-fifths of society.[1]

In the 1950's it became widely held that the progressive war and postwar taxation, plus the dispersion of shareholdings in financial institutions had undermined the economic base of an old style capitalist class which owned the means of production. In the 1960's it also was widely assumed that the rise of the investment funds had forwarded what the insurance companies the pension funds had not completed, and that ownership of capital had become a widely based phenomenon in a shareholding democracy.

But in fact, personal or individual holdings of shares still account for nearly *half* total shareholdings. And within these personal holdings *half again* are owned by the richest one per cent of the people. Only about a *third* of total shares is held by the institutions such as insurance companies, pension funds and unit trusts. All income from wealth accrues to the top fifth of the population which constitute Barratt Brown's middle and upper class population as defined by occupation, and within this category, as shown in Figure 1, income from wealth is itself massively concentrated — the top 8 per cent of those liable to tax secure more than three quarters of all income from investment, and less than one per cent take more than a third.[2] The top 100 or so wealth holders own over a thousand times the wealth of the average working man.[3]

In other words, whether class is defined by occupation or income, both divide the country between an upper and middle class including a fifth of taxpayers, and a working class which includes the remaining four-fifths of the population. It is mainly this top fifth of the population which invests in the private sector companies in Britain. This is illustrated in Figure 2, which shows that twenty one per cent of all taxpayers own *all* investment income.

As is well enough known, the Labour Party has many middle class supporters. Many of the most active among these are socialists. They frequently are the children of working class people, serious about the re-distribution of wealth, and anxious to support Labour policies radical enough to get to the root of stagnant investment, rising prices and high unemployment. Many such middle class supporters of the Party are reluctant capitalists, in the sense that they are given no real choice under the prevailing structure of investment by life insurance or pension funds in the country.

But in practice such a middle class are not capitalists in the same sense as the upper class and its concentrated top echelons. For instance, the middle class is different from the upper class in terms of its relationship to private investment capital. For the upper class, capital and the income from it is a moveable

feast. It is a surplus of massive proportions which can be shifted
from one firm, investment trust or commodity to another in
order to maximise personal profits. For the middle class, income
from wealth sometimes takes this form (especially in investment
trusts) but for the most part is immobile. It normally is tied up
in a mortgage, life insurance policy or pension fund and not
available for 'playing the market'.

There is another important difference between the upper and
middle classes. For the upper class capital is mainly an inherited
and unearned surplus to be maximised. For the middle class it
is mainly invested savings from income, i.e. earned rather than
unearned, and by the individual rather than his ancestors. Also,
it serves a direct use for the earner and the family — buying a
home for the family (mortgage); providing for dependents (life
assurance policy), or providing for spendable income in retirement (pension scheme).

Traditionally, socialism has aimed at nothing less than the
abolition of class society. According to Anthony Crosland, this
was impossible. He defined socialism not as the transformation
of class society, but as a willingness to give "exceptional
priority to overcoming poverty, distress and social squalor".[4]
This was in line with the *Beveridge Report* and the concept of
the welfare state pioneered by the postwar Labour government,
even if it went considerably less far than the conviction of a key
architect of that welfare state achievement — Nye Bevan — who
never relaxed his conception of capitalism as a class society and
socialism as its transformation.

Thirty years after the war, it is clear that the hopes for a
planned welfare state have been severely compromised. One
reason lies in the nature of planning within a capitalist system.
Where planning attempts only to alleviate poverty, distress and
squalor, it will perpetuate the capitalist mechanisms which con-
tinually throw up such social injustice, rather than transcend
them. In particular, if planning is not *socialist* planning, aiming
to transform the dominance of capitalist production and capitalist motivation, it will maintain the kinds of class structure and
economic inequalities which are essential as incentives to the
maintenance of a capitalist system. Such incentives give rise to
a dichotomy between economic progress and *social* progress be-

cause the government lacks the means to intervene in such a way as to transform the process of growth and distribution in a capitalist society. This was the fate of the 1964-70 Labour government, which found itself forced to put economic priorities before social redistribution. It failed to grasp that social redistribution depended on socialist transformation, and therefore was forced to cut back on the very social expenditure which was supposed to alleviate injustice and inequality. For instance, as Brian Abel Smith has shown, before Labour came to power, between 1958 and 1964, public services expenditure went up by nearly 28 per cent. But the National Plan budgeted for an increase in expenditure on public services between 1964 and 1970 of only 25 per cent. And this was *before* the major expenditure cuts on public services in the deflation of July 1966.[5]

More recent figures show that the British public gets a highly unequal return both for and *from* that part of its income taxed by the State. Michael Meacher has shown that in 1971-2 the State conferred more than two and a half times as much assistance to the professional middle and upper middle class through tax relief for occupational pensions, life insurance, mortgages and child allowances than it did on supplements to State retirement pensions, local authority rent subsidies and general family allowances. As shown on the right-hand column of Figure 1, this amounts to a working class subsidy of the middle and upper classes. Thus in 1971-2, tax rebates to the middle and upper class totalled nearly £2,400 millions and supplements to State retirement incomes, local authority rent subsidies and family allowances only £900 millions. *The gain for the beneficiaries in private welfare schemes were between two and three times the gains to the recipients of public welfare.*

However, as Meacher puts it, even this "understates the imbalance between Exchequer aid to different classes according to need". Inland Revenue statistics for 1971 reveal that life assurance tax relief per recipient amounted to only £11 annually for those with incomes under £1,000 a year; to £16 for those with incomes between £1,000 and £2,000 a year; £43 annually for the £2,000 to £5,000 a year range; £120 annually for those with between £5,000 and £10,000 a year and no less than

£253 annually for those with incomes over £10,000 a year. Meacher comments

> "The government have never produced comparable information about the distribution of tax gratuities to contributors to occupational pension schemes or mortgages, but there is no reason to doubt that it resembles this pattern whereby those with incomes under £20 a week get half the average benefit, while those with incomes of £200 a week get twelve times more than the average benefit. This inversion of welfare state values, this concentration of resources on those in least need, has been growing steadily since 1948."[6]

Confirmation of this massive class bias in taxation and tax hand-back is given by Frank Blackaby, who has shown that the share of taxes and national insurance contributions in the average male worker's pay packet more than doubled between 1963 and 1974, from 8.8 per cent to 21.1 per cent.[7]

In effect, the tax and welfare basis of the so-called Welfare State massively erode the living standards of the working class relative to the middle and upper classes.

This is at a time when the subsidy from the public to the private sector of industry has been running at astronomic daily rates — from £8 millions to £10 millions per working day (as shown later in this text).

In practice, granted the fact that the private shareholdings in the private sector are owned by the middle and upper classes, such public subsidy amounts to working class subsidy of the already privileged classes in society. This process is illustrated in the central column of Figure 1.

Such class bias is no accident. It stems essentially from the structure of power and unequal incomes necessary for the functioning of a capitalist system based on massively unequal rewards as the so-called incentive to efficiency.

This cannot be overcome through more fiddling with tax rates and indirect incentives by the government. It can only be transformed through a radical equalisation of wealth, a socialist programme for public ownership and control of the means of production, and new social controls of the expenditure and use of enterprise in the transformed system.

There are some people who maintain that this is nothing to do with Labour's manifestoes. But these are the 'pseudo-manifestists' who hesitate to challenge the inequality, inefficiency and injustice stemming from capitalism itself. They seek to mystify working people by abuse of the manifestoes and the Programme.

For in practice, such a socialist programme for new public enterprise and social control lies at the heart of the new direction in Labour Party policy since 1970, as any reference to the published texts of Party documents or this book will clearly demonstrate.

CHAPTER TWO

The State and Economic Power

The new direction to Labour's policies in the early 1970's was no accident. It reflected a widespread awareness that something very basic was wrong with the British economy. In the immediate postwar period it was widely held that the Keynesian revolution not only had solved the problem of mass unemployment, but had made feasible an indirect control of the economy itself. It was argued that if the State secured control of the level of aggregate demand, the profit motive and private self-interest would ensure the response of an efficient supply of goods and services in the public interest.

This was the essence of the Keynesian distinction between 'macro' and 'micro' economics. This new orthodoxy maintained that the State need exercise economic power only over the macro-economic factors (greek: macros — large). According to the Keynesian claims, the individual firm or company was not powerful. It was generally too small to influence the overall activity of the economy (greek: micros — small). In exceptional cases, it was argued, a particular firm could secure power over consumers through a monopolistic or dominant position in the market. But in general this would be restrained through national and international competition. Such competition would keep profits and prices at a 'normal' level over the long run.

Keynes clearly saw his theory of macro economic intervention as a means whereby the capitalist organisation of production would 'come into its own'.[8] The power of his insight into public management of *demand* was dramatic. It not only swept academic thinking, but also challenged the socialist claim that only public management of *supply* could ensure economic efficiency and social justice. It implied that, subject to a general role as spender, umpire and planner, and within a general framework of progressive taxation, the State could achieve the ends of socialism with only a limited degree of socialisation of ownership.

This proved a fundamental link between Keynesian thought and postwar social democratic thinking. It is clear that social democracy as expressed, for example by Anthony Crosland, has represented something more than Keynesian demand management plus progressive taxation and social concern. But reliance on macro-policy as the main area for the exercise of State economic power has remained a feature of social democratic thinking.

For example, in his major work *The Future of Socialism* Crosland claimed that "there is now no insuperable *economic* difficulty about the government imposing its will, provided it has one, on either public or private industry". He admitted that planners might be expected to have a better idea than private industry of the future rate of growth of the economy as a whole, and that industry might not be willing to shoulder the risks of expansion. But he claimed that planning could not be generalised for the whole economy. For one thing, he thought that there were few divergences between production for use and production for profit in the modern capitalist economy, and therefore relatively few cases where private benefits resulted in public costs. He could only cite two cases where this might occur — the balance of payments and regional development — and concluded "it will be seen how little can be said (on planning) in general terms". He was against "too much detailed planning *within* each sector", and claimed that "remaining severely empirical, the government must simply stand ready first to intervene negatively to stop industry from acting manifestly against the public interest: secondly, and of far greater importance, to search out the weak spots, especially in the basic industries, and concentrate on these with all the vigour at its command". In general Crosland saw the problem of planning as political, by which he essentially meant personal. He claimed that the 1945-51 experience showed that "those ministers prepared to plan could do so effectively", and that "if socialists want bolder planning they must choose bolder

ministers". Such ministers would be armed by the fiscal policies available to modern governments, plus subsidies, bulk pur-
chases and guarantees, which would remove the element of
risk from private enterprise and ensure that long term expansion
would be maintained.[9]

After the 1964-70 experience most of this looks very dated.
One could hardly have asked for a bolder planning minister
than George Brown, but no amount of personality could prevent
his plan from being suffocated before its first birthday by the
deflationary measures of July 1966. The claim that governments
are strong enough to impose their will on either private or public enterprise looks sad to pathetic after the admission in the
DEA 'After-Plan' *The Task Ahead,* which bluntly admitted in
1969 that "what happens in industry is not under the control
of the government".[10] The claim that fiscal policies will ensure
a sound balance of payments, investment expansion and
greater regional balance looks tragic after their use in 1966
to dig a hole in the heart of the economy and cut back expenditure on a scale which meant half a million unemployed by
1970, nearly double any previous level since the war.

The plain fact is that Labour lost the 1970 election on the
social democratic policies it had attempted in 1964. It can
claim that it inherited a balance of payments deficit of unprecedented dimensions. But in practice that deficit first mesmer-
ised and then paralysed it. And this lesson is doubly important
in the mid seventies, when the current account deficit including
invisibles and the increased price of oil promises a deficit some
five times the 1964 level.

Put differently, the Labour government's intentions from
1964 to 1970 may not have been in doubt, but its capacity to
control the economy was always in question. Its National
Plan started in a statistician's dreamworld and ended in the
nightmare of deflation. Because it lacked instruments for
directly sustaining expansion focussed on exports — through
new public enterprise in the export sectors — it had to use
fiscal measures and public expenditure cuts to restrain expansion itself. As a result, Labour from 1966 cut back on the
growth of income from which more could have been spent on
housing, health, education, pensions or helping the lower paid.

Since 1970, the Labour Party has come to question the permanence of the 'Keynesian revolution'. The awareness of this need stemmed partly from the deflationary package of July 1966 which ended the expansionary hopes of the National Plan, and with it most of the hopes for a planned re-distribution of income and increase in welfare on which the 1964 government had come to power. But the new awareness stemmed also from the patent failure of the efforts 1970-74 Conservative government to promote a sustained increase in investment supply through management of demand, and a realisation that the British economy was facing a degree of crisis unprecedented since the early thirties.

The 1974 Labour government inherited an economy gripped by rates of inflation which may reach twenty per cent a year; an astronomic deficit on the visible balance of trade (even excluding the massive cost of increased oil imports); a level of unemployment which would have been considered intolerable or unnecessary in the halcyon days of Keynesian orthodoxy in the fifties; a major imbalance in the regional distribution of that unemployment, concentrated in areas which hitherto have been traditionally Labour, but now are susceptible to the siren tones of Scots and Welsh nationalism; financial markets almost totally divorced from the needs of industrial development, with lament from the captains of industry that major firms in the economy are valued lower than empty office blocks; rising costs in personal borrowing, and house prices which have moved a mortgage beyond the reach of many potential buyers, and acted as a disincentive to further private house building. And this is all in addition to a 'floating' pound which has sunk steadily in relation to our main industrial competitors, aggravating the balance of payments deficit and domestic inflation, while failing to promote a sustained expansion of exports over imports.

CHAPTER THREE

The Trend to Monopoly

Such crisis in the British economy reflects a fundamental change in the structure of modern capitalism. This is one of the key themes in the Labour Party's 1973 Programme.

Diagrams 3 and 4 show that in 1970 the top hundred manufacturing firms in Britain had controlled some half of manufacturing output. In 1950 they had controlled only a fifth, and in 1910 only 1·5 per cent. On any reasonable projections, the top hundred are likely to proceed from strength to super-strength, and control two thirds of manufacturing around 1980.[11] Newbould and Jackson have made even more dramatic speculation that in the foreseeable future, unless countervailing action is taken, *three quarters* of the non-nationalised sector of British industry could be controlled by as few as *twenty-one* private companies.[12]

Such companies span the previous gap between micro and macro economic theory. The competitive firm of micro-economic theory was too small to influence macro-economic aggregates such as national investment, trade, and employment. Even in collusion, it was generally held, they could not seriously influence the price level set by sovereign consumers. Such theory still has relevance to the thousands of small companies which the giants are squeezing into the bottom half of industry. But *in between* these micro-economic firms and the macro-economic level of government policy, the new giants have introduced an intermediate or *meso*-economic sector.[13]

Put more simply, these are the big league firms which now command the heights of British industry and dominate the thousands of small league firms.

Table 1 shows just how monopolistic the top companies

are in British private industry. In fifteen of the twenty two main Industrial and Service Sectors in the economy, four firms or less control more than half of the total industry's assets. In twenty of the twenty two main industries and service sectors fewer than six firms control half of the assets.

The difference between the big and small firms in the private sector can be well illustrated by the construction industry. While there are some 100,000 small firms in the lower half of the construction industry, the top half of the industry is controlled by only 5 giant companies.

This is a situation of totally unequal competition. Most of the big firms in the top hundred are leaders or potential leaders in terms of prices, investment, innovation, job creation, trade and so on. When one of them moves with a new product or a raised price the rest of the big firms in the industry will follow suit. The small firms crowding into the bottom of the market are generally laggards in terms of scale of investment, innovation and productivity. But they gratefully follow the leaders in one key respect — the raising of prices once the leaders have set a new higher price level.

Raising prices has always been the prerogative of the monopoly. It is a key feature of their private power and public irresponsibility.

Under the capitalist structure of the turn of the century, as sketched in Figure 3, the consumer could choose between many firms in the top half of any given industry or market, and this tended to keep prices down. But now the consumer has little choice, unless he also is a big industrial firm with a market large enough to get good terms from leaders in other industries.

The housewife has virtually no choice at all, however much she shops around. For one thing, as shown in Table 1, the top six retailers control more than half the market power in retail trade. Their gains from size in distribution (economies of scale) are so enormous that they have lower costs than the shop on the corner. But this means that they can charge the same price as the small family retailer yet make a much higher profit. The grocer owning and running his own shop may well be squeezed and find it hard to make a living. But when only 14 wholesalers have more than half the muscle to raise prices in wholesaling (see Table 1), it is not surprising that the small scale retailer is himself complaining about inflation.

Table 2 shows that the joint monopoly power of the big league firms is even greater than half the market. In key foods and household goods two to three firms between them control from 80% to 95% of the goods in the shops. Also, in foods such as frozen fish and vegetables, soups, margarine, coffee, detergents and soaps it frequently is the same big league firm which dominates the market.

The phoney price competition of some of the big retailing chains shows in the extent to which they offer price bargains on some products this week which a fortnight later — without the same window dressing announcement — are back to their previous price, or more probably at a yet higher price. Even the 'special brands' offered by some retail chains are not really value for money in most cases. When instant potato, instant coffee or powdered milk is offered lower than the leading brand name prices, this still means a very high profit for most own-brand retailers simply because the leaders are in many cases making an astronomic profit on the brands.

The top 100 firms have now created a new domination over the mode of production, distribution and exchange in the heartland of the British economy. In practice they do not have to act collusively in order to act like a monopolist. Much of the same effect is secured through the mechanism of price leadership. Under competitive capitalism this used to mean a restraint of price increases. A market composed of many small firms, with low capital costs and easy entry to new markets, meant that if a single producer raised his price over a level which could give a competitor a profit, the competitor or new entrant would produce and sell at the lower price and attract consumers to himself and from the price leader. But under the new conditions of monopolistic domination of the major part of markets by a few firms, the main trend in pricing is up rather than down. When a leader firm has established a new higher price, the other large firms in the industry tend to follow suit rather than compete on price.

There are various reasons for this. One is the fear with which large companies view price competition. Like capitalist growth itself, such competition tends to prove highly unstable. There is no saying where it will end, especially if profit margins for the leaders in the industry are substantial. Such instability is anathema for leading firms under modern conditions, in part because the costs of applying new technology rise disproportionately over time, involving the advance planning of investment and production over several years. Such leading firms need market security in order to survive as leaders, and one of the most crucial forms of such security is a constant increase in the prices which they can charge to the consumer. They will compete in peripheral areas of the market where the mutual costs and gains may be marginal — such as advertising or minor differences in product and service. But even here they will do so mainly in those areas where the costs of such pseudo competition can be passed on to the consumer through higher prices.

But there are other reasons for the upward trend in pricemaking by the new leader firms in the private sector. One is the need to shelter smaller firms under a rising price umbrella. Unequal size aggravates unequal competition *unless price competition is basically suspended.* Such inequalities are found not only in production economies of scale or gains from size, but also in scale economies in management specialisation, access to finance, hold over suppliers and distributors, the size and throughput in firms' own distribution outlets at home and abroad, and so on. In general such gains reduce the costs of larger firms and therefore give them higher profits relative to smaller firms. When smaller firms are making a 'normal' profit, the big league firms in general will make 'super-normal' profits.

If the large firms were forced to price competitively in response to consumer wants, they would tend to reduce prices over the long run, transferring the gain from their lower costs through to the consumer in the form of lower prices. Smaller firms which did not benefit from such lower costs would not be able to earn a normal profit in such circumstances and would go out of business.

But one of the ironies of State intervention under monopoly trend conditions is a reversal of this normal profit and price sequence. Basically, the State has not yet caught up with the new monopoly domination of production, distribution and exchange. It is still trapped in a liberal capitalist ideology which maintains that if competition does not work through to prices this is the result either of exceptional factors such as collusion, or the outcome of events beyond the State's control such as rising prices for raw materials and imported commodities.

In wholesaling, the big companies are not slow to claim that there has been a massive increase in world commodity prices which has forced their own price up to retailers, and thus to the shopper. But while some commodity prices abroad have risen, this has been massively aggravated by capitalist speculation here at home in Britain. In the year before the February 1974 general election cocoa, copper and tin prices rose by more than 100 per cent. Sugar prices more than doubled, and other prices, in some cases jumped by more than double.

The reduced living standard for ordinary people, came from what John Palmer, Business Editor of *The Guardian* called "alarming evidence . . . that the activity of speculators on the London commodity market has played a major role in worsening both the rate of inflation and the balance of payments". Palmer's evidence is so damning it is worth citing further. As he put it, "One estimate in the City suggested that in some cases as much as *half* the increase in prices of some commodities last year (1973) was caused by speculative buying . . . Large firms, banks and wealthy private investors have been seeking investments to beat the cost of living and there also has been the unpredictability of currency movements, which were a speculators' favourite last year".

In simple terms, what this means is that because of the speculation of big firms, banks and the super rich some prices in the shops which were soaring in the early 1970's could have risen by *half* as much had it not been for the greed of the economically strong and the upper class. This freedom for a minority of the people to depress the living standards of the majority is the kind of power for private enterprise which Aims of Industry is trying to maintain that working people should defend.

The governments of Western Europe and the United States have increasingly resorted to price controls in an attempt to substitute for the failure of capitalism to ensure competitive prices. They also have reinforced anti-monopoly or anti-trust agencies which have sought to prevent abuses of competition.

Yet in practice, such State intervention to impose a liberal capitalist mode of behaviour in an era of rising monopoly has perverse and contradictory results. Even if the State prices policy attempts only to *restrain* the rate of prices increases, rather than to impose a freeze, this will tend to squeeze the profit margins of smaller companies more than the higher profits of larger firms. In practice this will result either in an acceleration of their takeover by larger firms, or their protest and pressure through trade associations on the government to relax its policy.

This is one of the reasons for the stop-go nature of State prices policy. But over the long run both the pressure of trade associations and the intervention of anti-monopoly agencies will promote other contradictions when governments try to maintain a liberal capitalist mode of production under monopoly conditions. For instance, there is no doubt that anti-monopoly agencies in general are vigilant and bite hard on monopoly abuse whenever ministers or governments permit. But the possibility that mergers will not be allowed or that major companies actually might be broken up prompts long term pricing policies by leading firms which are designed to keep clear of the anti-monopoly agencies.

This means that leading firms maintain a relatively regular increase in prices not only in order to swell their own profits, but also to preserve a more normal profit level over the long run in higher cost and less competitive smaller firms. This both keeps the smaller firms quiet and allows the larger firms to finance their own relatively greater internal growth through some of the retained abnormal profits. Variations on this theme occur from time to time. But they are generally in favour of the big league leaders, who may sometimes hold prices stable during a period of rising costs in such a way as to soften up a medium sized competitor for takeover. In such a case the game is likely to be called off before the anti-monopoly agency is called in, with a suitably profitable bid made for the absorbed company from the abnormal profits of the larger firm.

Such unequal competition *means a reversal of the whole basis of profit and pricing in the competitive capitalist model.* In terms of the conceptual framework or ideology of liberal capitalism, the consumer is served through price competition which means that new entrants can pull prices down if a monopoly leader tried to push them up to swell its profits over and above the 'norm' for the industry. But in the first place the big league firms in most cases are too secure to be challenged by even a medium sized company. Also, partly in order to avoid the teeth of the anti-monopoly agencies, they tend to set their prices at a level which ensures the survival of less efficient firms in the economy.

In such a way the prices in modern capitalism tend to be set by the most efficient firms, as in the liberal capitalist model. But they are set at a level determined by the costs of the least efficient firms which the leaders wish to survive. The trend to larger leader size and monopoly has stood the price, profit and consumer welfare assumptions of liberal capitalism on its head.

These are not the only reasons for the 'new inflation' which either perplex theorists looking in the wrong place, or confound their case that unions alone are responsible for inflation.

One of the major reasons for dramatic recent inflation relates to a change in the structure of the modern capitalist firm itself.

Under small scale capitalism, a high proportion of the investment needs of firms were met by share subscriptions taken up on the stock market. This meant that during expansion of the trade cycle, when demand rose and goods became scarce relative to supply, firms made higher profits and passed them on at least in part to shareholders.

Inversely, when demand for products fell during contraction of trade in the cycle, profits fell and shareholders had less distributed to them. If necessary they got nothing for a while, until profits began to flow in again.

But the rise of managerial capitalism on a major scale has changed this. In other words, the management of big league firms has become increasingly concerned not to lose boardroom control to shareholders. They have not worried about the impotent if parasitic small shareholders for some time. Their shares have been too dispersed, and their shareholders' action too disorganised, to pose much of a threat to management.

What has increasingly concerned management in the big league has been the big personal shareholder with the vast inherited upper class fortune, and the big institutional shareholders (insurance companies and pension funds representing middle class savings).

The institutional shareholders to date have exercised very little positive control over big league management. But they can have a negative effect both on the reputation of management and the finances of the company by moving their funds out when they dislike the way the company is being run. The same is broadly true of the big personal shareholders, though in many cases their specialist advisers take a more direct interest in company management.

As a result, big league firms have increasingly resorted to external borrowing to finance major projects at home or abroad.

Under the relatively sustained growth of the twenty years after the war, the big league firms became used to sustained profits. They therefore became less worried about financing their need for extra capital through fixed interest borrowing such as bank loans or bond issues.

This was especially true during the 1960's, in which the big league increasingly went multinational in operation and borrowed on the Eurodollar and Eurobond markets.

As analysed in the following chapter, the unequal competition between big firms in the multinational sector and small national firms gave the big league a great advantage in such external finance, which was not available to smaller, less secure and therefore less creditworthy firms.

But the bliss only lasted so long as the system itself expanded in some relatively balanced way. In the present crisis and the recession of demand in key countries, the big league price leaders have found that they have to pay their costs of borrowing at fixed rates of interest despite the fall in sales. Therefore they have tended to raise prices to maintain their cash-flow and profits over and above borrowing costs.

This is illustrated by the fact that the General Motors corporation in the United States recently *in*creased prices when demand for big cars fell following the OPEC oil price increases.

Put differently, share finance had the advantage that in lean years shareholders could be passed over and told to wait. But Eurodollar and Eurobond bankers, who normally combine in big syndicates for loan issues, are more powerful and less patient.

As a result, the rise of big league meso-economic power has been accompanied by a reversal of the main price sequence in the capitalist trade cycle. The cycle used to show rising prices during expansion and falling prices during recession. Now it shows rising prices during *both* expansion *and* recession.

But these are not the only reversals in the role of price and profits in the capitalist orthodoxies. As profoundly, the system of *inter*national trade and payments which predominated after the war has been reversed by a new *multi*national trade and payments system.

This contradiction of classic capitalist ideology has further major consequences for the role of State intervention and democratic power in countries such as Britain.

CHAPTER FOUR

The Multinational Dimension

Between the wars, international trade was genuinely international. It took place almost exclusively between different firms in different countries. Such firms were significantly influenced by changes in exchange rates imposed by their home governments, since this would affect the price at which they sold on competitive markets abroad.

For some time after the war, exchange rate changes on Keynesian lines had a very considerable influence on the international competitiveness of enterprise. They have not been a panacaea, any more than Keynes imagined that they would be if not backed by supplementary national and international policies. Nor have they been able to offset the massive dynamism of strong versus weak points in the world capitalist system. Continual revaluations of the Deutschmark have not stemmed the trade surplus of West Germany over the long term any more than the devaluation and downwards floating of sterling since 1967 has meant a long term improvement in Britain's trade competitiveness.

In general, despite Keynes' analysis of what could be done by the nation state to help itself in foreign trade, backed by international agencies, it is widely recognised that something is very wrong with the world international trade and payments system. Individual commentators stress particular weaknesses — the link of international monetary arrangement to the dollar, and the failure to establish an international credit unit of the more neutral kind which Keynes himself wanted — the Bancor. Other commentators stress mistiming or mismanagement in the world trade and payments system, both by national governments and by international agencies.

But it is increasingly clear to many people that something much more fundamental has changed since Keynes and the interwar period. Moreover, it has happened recently and at an accelerating rate which has taken many governments by surprise. This is the increasing substitution of a predominantly *inter*national system of trade and payments between firms and countries by a *multi*national trade and payments system. Put more directly, a system in which most trade is conducted between different firms in different countries is giving way to a system in which trade increasingly is conducted between the *same* big league firms in different countries. This fundamental difference between international and multinational trade underlies the increasing threat which multinationals can pose to national economic sovereignty.

The problem partly lies in the fact that the big league firms which already dominate the domestic British economy are themselves multinationals, and can use their power to locate investment and jobs outside Britain to bargain terms which suit them more than the government for their operation in Britain. This is a considerable sanction. In trade terms it means a rise in British imports from the foreign venture unless the government either selectively controls imports from the company abroad or develops its own import substituting capacity in the product concerned through other means.

But an essential part of the problem posed by the new multinationals lies in the extent to which they can suspend the normal constraints and incentives of the price mechanism in transactions between their subsidiaries in different countries. In such transactions these companies are *their own* main market. By trading between subsidiaries *they side-step* the market mechanism underlying Keynesian international trade models. To the extent that their domestic market hold in individual countries represents a situation of joint or shared monopoly, they also are not subject to the range of competitive constraints at home which used to characterise a market situation. In other words, their multinational activity is a global dimension reinforcing the big league meso-economic power which they now exercise in the home market.

According to Anthony Crosland, "the multinational trend

may have passed its peak".[14] Yet Crosland gives no quantitative evidence to back this optimism. A Harvard Business School analysis of the top 100 firms by Derek Channon found evidence of "a dramatic increase" in multinational operations between 1960 and 1970, and effectively all the top 100 firms are multinationals.[15]

The main ways in which multinational companies erode government economic sovereignty were outlined in the Labour Party Opposition Green Paper on *The National Enterprise Board*.[16] Basically, multinational operation means that leading companies increasingly choose to locate investment abroad and use foreign labour in production rather than export abroad from their home market. In this way international trade between different companies in different countries has increasingly been replaced by multinational trade between the same companies in different countries.

This can damage the economic sovereignty of the home country or a high tax welfare state economy in several ways.

First, multinational companies charge themselves high import prices from subsidiaries abroad in excess of the price which would be charged under competitive international trade. In other words, while the import price in international trade might amount to x pounds sterling, the multinational will charge itself x plus y per cent from a foreign subsidiary. This practice (i) reduces the delcared profits of the British branch of the multinational while raising the profits of the foreign branch, with the transaction frequently passing through a holding company in a foreign tax haven; (ii) thereby reduces the tax paid by the multinational and erodes the tax resources for social expenditure available to the government in Britain; (iii) artificially raises the value of British imports over and above the x pounds sterling price which would have been paid under competitive international trade conditions.

In effect, control over the prices charged on imports from subsidiaries abroad is crucial to countervailing multinational power in the Category 1 big league sector — all of which are multinational in opeiation. Transfer pricing through imports, hits the balance of payments (through inflating the value — price — of imports while not increasing the usefulness of the goods), domestic prices (raised because of inflated imports) and tax revenue (reduced through the entering of inflated imports as costs rather than profits to the multinational as a whole).

As critically, for unions, *such transfer pricing in multinational trade weakens union wage bargaining power* by under-stating real profits made in the UK. This is why the provisions in the August 1974 White Paper *The Regeneration of British Industry* for revelation to unions of the value of both exports *and* imports in the Category 1 big league is a crucial condition for their effective wage bargaining.

For the same reasons, such revealed information is a critical necessary condition for the use of the Planning Agreements system as a selective form of *import controls and balance of payments saving*. Without such information, the government can only use general import controls for all firms, which not only contravene GATT rules, but are less effective than selective controls in the big league multinationals which now dominate the upper half of our economy, and disproportionately dominate our international trade.

Second, multinational companies not only can damage the domestic balance of payments through inflating imports in order to transfer profits abroad, but tend to erode the effectiveness of devaluation or a downwards floating of the currency as an instrument of increasing for foreign price competitiveness of exports. The reasons here are simpler but still important. Multinational companies frequently produce and sell substitutable products in different countries. As already shown, market security is important for them to be able to plan the large scale investments over several years which are involved in a given product range. They therefore tend to reduce international competition between their own subsidiaries to peripheral areas of the market. Car firms operating in several countries will allow imports from their subsidiaries abroad, but normally at higher cost than their domestic substitutes. When a national currency is devalued, they will not normally reflect the full decrease in the foreign price of exports in their sales abroad for fear of undermining their production and sales in that country.

Third, multinational companies can erode the effective-

ness of government credit policies by their privileged access
to multinational capital. For instance, the Eurodollar market
involves a relative high rate of fluctuation in borrowing costs
for those consortia of international banks which operate it.
Only those firms guaranteed long term survival and profits
through their multinational size (or public ownership) are
sufficiently credit-worthy for such loans. As a result the
competitive small league firms bounded within national markets rarely gain access to such finance, and are hard enough
bitten by government credit restrictions during inflationary
periods. But the big league multinationals can by-pass domestic
credit restrictions through their access to such international
financial markets.

Fourth, multinational companies can aggravate the balance
of payments position of a national economy and bring pressure
on its strained currency through hedging or speculating against
it on a larger scale than national companies. They also can
arrange the timing of their multinational transactions between subsidiaries in such a way as to maximise their own
cash gains when a currency has been devalued, while thereby
promoting the very devaluation from which they benefit.[17]

One of the reasons for the syphoning of profits abroad
through the x plus y technique of transfer pricing is the wide
range over which prices in trade between subsidiaries can be inflated without attracting the attention of national tax authorities. The price of final products sold abroad is clearly published
and readily available. But multinationals are their own guardians
of the real cost of production or transformation of the raw
materials, commodities and components in trade between their
own subsidiaries.

This distinction between published profits and real profits is
crucial in understanding the way in which multinational companies have come to secure a monopolistic hold on the markets
of the mature capitalist economies. They have a virtual monopoly of information on what their real profits actually are. In
practice, the declared profits of big league companies in Britain
and other economies in which multinationals mainly sell their
goods are not much out of line with profits of smaller firms
bound mainly to the domestic market. In some cases, medium

and small firms can register profits which actually are higher than those declared by multinationals.[18]

But as the previous argument indicates, there is a vital difference between profits declared to the tax authorities and the profits earned by multinationals and shunted abroad through the technique of transfer pricing (high import prices from subsidiaries abroad). It has already been shown that the leading companies in the big league sector of the economy set prices at a level which allows less efficient smaller companies to survive. It is not surprising that the normal or limited profit schedules of these smaller firms are taken by multinationals as the norm at which they are prepared to declare tax to the Inland Revenue. In practice the tax authorities have virtually no way of countering this multinational monopoly of information on costs and profits. This stems from the fact that multinationals purposely divide production in various stages in different countries round the world, or frequently are their own providers of raw materials and commodities for import and transformation in the mature economies in which final sales will be made.

The tax authorities in the developed capitalist economies would be hard put to trace this multinational division of costs and profits even if they could spare the resources to do so. Even the energy of the Prices and Incomes Board under the last Labour government drew a blank when it came to attempting to devise guidelines for the pricing policies of multinational companies. As Mr. Aubrey Jones bluntly put it, a method "of determining objectively what is a 'proper' rate of profit might be possible if more were known about the problem as seen from the standpoint of multinational companies . . . (But) the Board was able to touch only on the fringe of this enormous issue in two cases . . ."[19] The same kind of problem faced the Tory government when it discovered the astronomic profit which Roche was making on the sale of librium and valium to the National Health Service. This arose from vigorous work by a member of the Monopolies Commission who discovered that the price of these drugs in the Italian private sector was several *thousand* per cent lower than that charged to the National Health Service by Roche.

The Inland Revenue had no idea of the scale of the profits which were being syphoned abroad by Roche, not least because it had no direct knowledge of research and production costs of the kind which now could be revealed through public ownership and an opening of the books to workers through the Planning Agreements system.

The lessons are clear. In both domestic and international policy the modern capitalist State is plunged increasingly in the dark by the simultaneous trend to monopoly domination at home and multi-nationalism abroad. Keynesian policies are increasingly eroded both by the increased market power and self financing of the big league at home, and by their capacity to thwart government taxation, monetary and exchange rate policies. Prices in Britain and the other mature capitalist economies are increasingly decided by that level which leading companies determine as sufficient to maintain smaller and less efficient companies in being, while disguising the abnormal profits secured through their own increasing gains from size and multinational spread.

CHAPTER FIVE

Public Money in the Private Sector

The British public so far has been getting very bad value for money which the government spends on its behalf in the private sector. The State expenditure which subsidizes the private sector does not 'generate' the sustained growth of investment jobs and income in the manner of procreative Keynesian metaphors. The money is pumped in on a massive scale, but the result is largely barren.

Over the years the public subsidy of the private sector has assumed massive dimensions. It has been estimated by Michael Barratt Brown that by the late 1960's it was amounted to nearly 7 per cent of national product, and *nearly equivalent to half of all private sector fixed capital formation* excluding housing. This included public subsidies for agriculture, capital grants and investment allowances, technical services provided to the private sector by the State including research and development aid, incentives for local employment, wage subsidies through the Regional Employment Premium, and so on.[20] Expressing the subsidy differently, Mervyn King of the Cambridge Department of Applied Economics has calculated that the cumulative effect of capital grants, investment allowances and employment premia since the early 1950's has been *equivalent to half company taxation.*[21]

But these are not the only ways in which public money subsidizes profits in the private sector. Enormous subsidies to private enterprise accrue through government reluctance to cover costs from receipts in the public sector industries which sell them steel and service them with power, transport infrastructure, and post and telecommunication services. As argued more fully in a later chapter, the pattern of public sector losses is not inevitable or a reflection of lower efficiency in the public than the private sector. Richard Pryke has shown that during the 1960's, by which time long term planning after the postwar nationalisations had time to take effect, labour productivity in the publicly owned industries was uniformly higher than in privately owned manufacturing.[22] What actually has happened has been government restraint of prices in the public sector in an effort to restrain the rate of inflation in the economy as a whole. This is based on the outdated ideology that private manufacturing is basically price competitive and will pass on such subsidies from the public sector to the private consumer in the form of lower prices. Essentially, any public sector corporation, like any private company, can make a profit if it is able to push up prices to its consumers. In practice, for the above reasons and through hesitation in tackling the price-making power of the private big league firms, governments have held back public sector prices and thereby subsidised profits in the private firms which overall have pushed up prices to the consumer rather than restrained or reduced them.

Estimates of the value of such subsidy to the private sector through public sector losses have been made for 1972-3, and total some £400 million to £500 million a year. A similar figure can be added to this for government subsidy of research and development. The public-subsidy through grants, free depreciation, investment allowances and employment premia, equivalent to halving true company taxation gives a gross public subsidy of the private sector on these items alone of some £1,300 millions subsidy from a total £2,600 millions levied through Corporation Tax. Adding up these items alone gives a public subsidy to the private industrial sector of £2,100 millions to £2,300 millions a year or *£8 million to £9 million per working day.*[23]

This process of public subsidy of the private sector, and therefore *working class subsidy of the middle and upper-class shareholders,* is illustrated in Figure 1.

For small firms such aid in many cases is important in maintaining both profitability and survival. But there is evidence that such small firms benefit least from State subsidy, not only because they are now in the shrinking lower end of industry, but also because they are less efficient at organising their way through the maze of government administration which channels it.

This is not the only way in which the present public subsidy to the private sector benefits those big firms which need it least. As Geoff Wood, Director of the Sheffield Centre for Innovation and Productivity puts it, "the system automatically favours the bigger companies". He gives the example of a big league firm with multinational operations which will ensure public subsidy of most of its operations in the following way. It claims investment grants of up to 22 per cent on buildings and plant for a project in a Development Area. It then claims up to 100 per cent of the cost of its capital equipment against corporation tax, which under present legislation is allowed during the first year of the asset's life. The new project may not make a profit which would be subject to corporation tax during that year, but the company claims and gets the subsidy for the equipment anyway through writing the cost off against the tax due from other profitably operating divisions. It ensures that it does not make too much profit in the UK on which it would have to pay corporation tax by shifting the profit to another country through selling products to one of its own subsidiaries or associates below cost. It also makes capital equipment in the government subsidised plant in a Development Area, which it sells to an associated group company anywhere in the country which can claim the standard 100 per cent write off against corporation tax.[24]

Evidence that the big firms in the top 100 league are unresponsive to public handouts is most evident where the handouts are biggest — on regional aids and incentives. Investment grants and labour subsidies for regional development constitute the biggest standard injection of public money to the private sector. Yet in recent evidence to the Commons Expenditure Committee Unilever submitted that "we are unable to produce evidence from our own experience that the Regional Employment Premium has increased investment of employment in the Development Areas".

Cadbury Schweppes submitted that neither labour nor capital incentives played a major role in location decisions.

GKN stated that "the attraction of the incentives has so far been inadequate". Tube Investments said that "there are not many projects where regional policy is of critical importance to the strategic decision (to locate)". Univac stated that "we would have gone to a Development Area regardless of the grants offered" and Dunlop frankly admitted that it made a surplus from regional aid which was useful for investment elsewhere.

This 'elsewhere' is increasingly abroad rather than in Britain at all. As the Burroughs Company submitted in the same evidence, it "along with other companies, is locating in Taiwan, Brazil, Mexico, the Philippines and Hong Kong, where the cost of labour is very low". When asked how low, the Financial Director of Burroughs replied that such foreign labour costs were about a quarter of those in Britain, and agreed with a member of the Commons Committee that "an employment premium would have to be very substantial to locate here (in Britain)".[25]

This is true enough. On labour costs alone, the Regional Employment Premium wage subsidy would have to be raised to *75 per cent* just to equalise wage costs in British Development ment Areas and Third World union and labour havens. And this does not take account of the massive gains which companies secure through transfer pricing between their multi-national subsidiaries, by which they charge themselves high import prices to the UK and thereby syphon income away from the Inland Revenue for expansion abroad. The several thousand per cent difference between the price charged by Roche on librium and valium in its sales to the National Health Service and the price offered by an Italian company may have been exceptional, but under present policy we have little or no way of knowing what scale of funds are being syphoned abroad by the multinational leaders. These companies have a monopoly of information on their own profit and cost structures which imposes lockjaw on the teeth of the taxman. This worsens the balance of payments as the multinational trend accelerates. At the same time it reduces the tax revenue available for public sector investment and wages, whether in public enterprise or housing, health, education and social services.

The lesson from this evidence is clear enough. If a government increases cash handouts to leading companies it will not overcome the hesitation of their management to undertake a broad wave of new investment in this country. The State incentives would melt like snow through the transfer pricing of multinational companies and mainly end up in investment elsewhere. At the same time this syphoning of cash abroad would *worsen* rather than improve the balance of payments, since it works through the artificial inflation of import prices, and the deflation or under-statement of the price of exports.

The problem poses no less of a challenge than that which Keynes tried to meet when faced with chronic unemployment between the wars. But is a problem which cannot be solved either through Keynesian demand management or through greater cash handouts to firms in the hope that they will increase investment. Some new projects would materialise as a result of the handout policy but nothing like sufficient to solve the investment on a major expansion of exports. In general, like Univac, the firms would accept the increased volume of public funds to subsidize what they would have done "regardless of the grants offered".

CHAPTER SIX

The Unmixed Economy

Socialist planning for social needs will depend on a new mix in the so-called mixed economy, and socialist criteria for the activities of new public enterprise.

The share of national product spent on public expenditure has been rising over the postwar period. It approached 50 per cent of total product in 1970. Much of this increase was a result of greater relative expenditure on social services by central and local government — i.e. education, health and welfare, social security and housing. The rest included aid to the existing public sector through subsidies and grants, and the capital formation costs of the nationalised industries.

But the striking feature of the main part of the existing public and private sectors is their separateness or virtual apartheid.

What we now have is essentially an *un*-mixed economy, with big league private enterprise command*ing* the heights of profitable manufacturing and services, and big league public enterprise command*ed* by what private enterprise demands from it.

Both public enterprise and public expenditure in Britain today are concentrated in basic industry, social services and economic and social infrastructure. These areas of the economy have been brought into public ownership because they are crucial for the success of the remaining sectors of the economy — essentially manufacturing industry and private sector services.

One of the problems for the British economy lies in the fact that while such a public sector base is a necessary condition for the success of the remaining sectors, it is not a sufficient condition. This stems from the fact that the full use and further expansion of the *existing* public sector depends on demand for goods, jobs and services generated in the private sector. At the same time, the generation of new income in the economy which can be spent on new social services also depends on the rate of growth of the private sector.

For instance, the publicly owned basic industries and services such as gas and electricity, rail transport, post office communications and steel are essentially *passive* or *growth dependent* sectors. They depend for the growth of their output and investment on the *active growth initiating* sectors of manufacturing and modern services. Expanding their capacity without a corresponding increase in the private manufacturing and service sectors would simply result in unused capacity and a waste of public resources.

This is one of the reasons why the existing public sector cannot be used by the government to generate a broad wave of investment and modernisation through the economy. But there are others. They concern the broad range of further constraints on balanced economic expansion including foreign trade, regional development and pricing.

For instance, with the exception of steel and coal little of the existing public sector can contribute to improving our notorious long term deficit on the visible balance of trade. We can't export British rail services, domestic power generation or domestic post office services. Similarly, and we should fully admit this, the public ownership of development land will not improve the trade balance (even if controls preventing the export of capital into property speculation abroad can help improve the balance of payments). By the same token, our public ownership of the ports may speed exports through increased efficiency, but also will speed up imports from abroad.

The same imbalance between the public and private sectors shows clearly in the problem of promoting greater equality between regions. With the exception of steel, which itself is shedding jobs rather than creating them, the existing public sector is location tied for geological, geographic or demographic reasons. Mining is tied to specific localities for geological reasons. Power distribution, public transport and post office communications are spread through the country to serve the public in particular localities and regions. The same is true of the bulk of the private service sector, which is tied up in the distribution of goods and services to particular areas. It is only manufacturing and head office services — still almost all in private ownership and control — which are really mobile between different regions.

But the imbalance or separateness of the public and private sectors in the economy is most marked in the area of prices. This phenomenon of unequal pricing is characteristic of the public sector through most of the mature capitalist economies, and has become more marked during the long-term trend to inflation through the last ten to fifteen years. Basically, governments have consciously held back public sector prices as a counter-inflation policy. This has made short-term sense in as much as the classic pattern of nationalisation in the mature capitalist countries has been concentrated in basic industries and services. If the private manufacturing and service sectors were essentially competitive, the lower cost of their inputs from the public sector might be transferred through to lower prices and increased export competitiveness.

But it now is patently clear both that pricing in the big league firms no longer is competitive, and that the short-term inflation has become long-term and is worsening year by year. As a result, government restraint of public sector prices amasses an enormous deficit. In 1972-3 this amounted to well over £1,400 millions. Such a deficit has to be financed either through taxation or through grants and write offs to the public sector which are not met by taxation and therefore aggravate the inflationary spiral. When that spiral coincides with a major balance of payments deficit, as happened in Britain in 1973 a capitalist government will cut public sector investment expenditure in the vain hope that this will check the long term problem. In practice, of course, it only aggravates it by decreasing the quality of public sector service, overloading existing plant and facilities, and undermining the investment flow in basic industry and services on which the economy in the long term depends.

Such policies are crucially demoralising for public sector management and workers. They force deficits on public industries and services through imposing prices which are too low to cover costs. This gives the public sector in general a 'poor relation' image in relation to the 'rich relation' of the private sector.

The image is, of course, projected to the public as consumer. In crude terms it is expressed in the common fallacy that public enterprise 'doesn't work'. Part of the fallacy stems from the very nature of some of the public sector services, which involve the congested use of specific facilities at unequally loaded times. This is especially clear in public transport congestion at commuter stations and in urban public transport. Such relative congestion at peak traffic times would in fact be inescapable for private enterprise companies — and indeed is for many private bus companies in urban transport. The public also frequently overlooks the fact that without private vehicle use of road transport at peak travel times the speed and quality of public sector transport could be massively increased.

However, the real 'poor relation' in the existing public sector is the wage earner. The post office workers, the rail workers (whether in national or urban transport), the municipal workers, the school teachers, the nurses and hospital staff, plus wide categories of those who work in social services and social security — these workers have become the new proletariat of the public sector.

The reason is simple enough. In a system which is dominated by commercial criteria and in which the public sector plays only a passive role in relation to the active private sector, it is inevitable that prices and wages should be led in the private sector and lag in the public sector.

Part of the key to this problem is the restraint of prices imposed on the public sector by governments which are futilely attempting to restrain inflation indirectly through restraint in the public sector, rather than directly — at source — in the price making power of the big league enterprise in modern manufacturing and services.

In other words, so long as the modern capitalist State

attempts to maintain a dual or separate system in which the
meso leaders are largely left free to make abnormal profits
and shunt them abroad the basic industries and services in
public ownership will pay the social costs.

Both wages and investment in the existing public sector
could be increased by allowing public enterprise to increase
its prices. *Any enterprise can pay its way provided it is given
sufficient price freedom,* and provided its market position will
not be eroded by price competition. The massive expansion
through internal growth and take-overs by the new giant companies shows this very clearly. But without either increased
taxation or an erosion of abnormal profits in the private
big league (which means countering their multinational profit
syphoning), such an increase in prices and wages in the existing public sector would be inflationary.

These are some of the reasons why a socialist government
should ensure a new mix in the so-called mixed economy.
But there are others. One is the need to ensure that the new
public sector is widely represented in job expansion rather than
the sectors of job loss and employment decline in which it so
far has been concentrated (coal, steel and rail transport). The
job loss syndrome reinforces the low prices, low wage and low
investment features of much of the existing public sector. It
not only makes recruitment and an age balanced labour force
more difficult, but also reinforces a defeatist 'poor relation'
psychology among some public sector workers and management.

CHAPTER SEVEN

Public Ownership of Leading Firms

The key case for public ownership and control of leading manufacturing enterprise lies in the scope which this opens for directly harnessing the power of big business and ensuring that it fulfils social and economic policy. If Labour in government follows the policy of taking over only failing firms there is no hope of harnessing such power. A lame duck National Enterprise Board of some half dozen bankrupt companies will hardly be able to deliver any of the results set out in Labour's Programme over even a five year period. Even an NEB of half a dozen substantial and viable companies will make relatively little impact over the range of economic objectives such as investment promotion, raised productivity, regional development, price restraint, contribution to exports and countervailance of multinational capital.

To secure the broad wave of investment through manufacturing industry on which so much else depends, new public enterprise must range through the principal manufacturing sectors. At present as illustrated in Figure 5, these are almost wholly under the control of big league private firms in the top 100 category. Within them, the new public enterprise must be represented in companies whose internal efficiency and scales is sufficient to match that of the remaining private sector leaders. In short, the new public enterprise must include actual or potential leaders in the big league sector. Otherwise, it cannot exert a new leadership under social control in the public interest.

If this initial package of companies is secured, the government through these companies can gain both a direct and indirect mobilisation of investment and resources. It can do so by promoting a new leadership in the scale of investment, rate of innovation and rate of productivity which the other front rank firms in the industry must follow or lose market share and volume profits to the new leaders. It thereby would prompt large scale, entirely new projects embodying major gains in technical progress of the kind which the British private sector has failed to deliver in this country since the war. If the new public enterprise is represented across the board in manufacturing as a whole, such a process also will result in (i) an upwards move in the rate of demand for goods and services in manufacturing and the private service sector, and (ii) in the existing public sector in basic industry and service which, as already shown, is dependent on private sector manufacturing and services for the growth of its own sales and productivity.

On the investment front, new public enterprise through the broad range of manufacturing can directly undertake investment projects which the private sector leaders have hesitated to promote for fear of ending with surplus capacity. It can push through the major plant and new equipment which will be essential if the government is not to be forced to accept a major deflation of the economy and massive unemployment.

Such public enterprise must range *through* manufacturing for two main reasons.

First, only such a broad range of new investment will ensure that the *push* effect of expanded investment is balanced and contributes to raising overall industrial capacity in the economy.

Isolated increases in investment can be useful in some industries, such as engineering, in which capacity was notably insufficient in the early seventies. But these cases will only bring such a sector into line with the existing overall rate of growth of industrial investment, rather than raise investment capacity through the economy as a whole.

Second, direct expansion of investment through new public enterprise can only harness the power of the big league private sector firms if it is represented in the main industrial sectors in which they operate. In other words, as illustrated in Figure 6, the push of the public enterprise leaders can only exert a *pull* effect on other big firms if the public enterprises are comparable with them in the first place in terms of size, technology and market power.

The dynamics of this pull effect are familiar enough in the boardrooms of leading private companies. In economic jargon, the pull amounts to oligopoly leadership, or the situation in which one of a few firms at the top end of an industry breaks from the pack and pioneers a new product or technique on a major scale. While the other leading firms otherwise might have hung around and delayed introducing a similar project or process, they cannot any longer afford to do so without risk of losing sales, profits and market share to the pioneer firm.[26]

It is clear that such a combined push and pull effect in the big league sector cannot be left to chance. If it is to prove effective in promoting the sustained growth of industrial capacity which has eluded governments relying on Keynesian demand management, such investment supply must be co-ordinated in a new planning framework for leading companies. The main potential of such a system of Planning Agreements is analysed in the following chapter. They include the widened scope for planning the spread of investment demand, jobs and incomes made possible through a higher rate of expansion by big league firms. In other words, instead of relying on a macro-economic multiplier or spread effect on Keynesian lines, such agreements would plan the multiplier at the crucial meso-economic level of the big league firms where investment response to Keynesian demand management has hitherto been so ineffective.

Nonetheless, as stressed in the following chapter, such new dimensions to economic planning cannot be ensured through Planning Agreements or coordination of big league firms alone. There has to be something wide ranging and new to coordinate in the first place. To achieve this it will not be sufficient for a government department to get together with the management and workers' representatives of leading companies through the Planning Agreements system and exhort them to increase the scale of investment. In itself such exhortation of the big league firms would be no more certain of success than the exhortation of the 1965 National Plan and the meetings of the industrial development committees.

A socialist policy must aim to manage the economy in the public interest as the basis for wider social transformation. To do this it must be able to harness the *strong* points of the system. This is where the spearheading function of new public enterprise is crucial in establishing a new public mix in the now almost exclusively private manufacturing sector.

In practice, this means securing ownership to achieve real control of leading enterprise in the big league manufacturing firms. It is only in the context of ownership that legislation requiring leading companies to take part in coordinated planning can prove effective. It is only in such a context that the full potential of the push on investment through public enterprise and the pull effect on private enterprise can result in a sustained increase in industrial capacity sufficient to match effective demand management.

Put differently, Keynesian demand management techniques have failed to ensure a focussed investment response in an economy where the market has increasingly been eclipsed by the rise of monopolistic big league power. An underlying reason for such a failure, as already stressed, lies in the increasing investment horizon necessary for large scale big league enterprise, which extends beyond the shorter cycle of stop-go budgets. Combined with easier investment opportunities in faster growing or lower wage cost economies abroad, this trend in the big league multinational sector has qualified the effectiveness of Keynesian demand management policies. The rise of this meso-economic power has divorced the big firm from the marriage with State power which Keynes blueprinted at the macro-economic level, and has undermined the application of his employment economies to the economics of growth and distribution. Only *extensive* new public enterprise in the big league sector can bridge this gap and ensure that demand management is wedded to an effective investment response. In short Keynes' limited socialisation at the macro-economic level must be complemented under new conditions by a more extended socialisation of the big league firms which now dominate half the economy.

In regional development, new public enterprise ranged through manufacturing could give a Labour government the

means to transform the present inequalities in jobs and employment not only between major regions, but also within particular areas and localities. Manufacturing, with head office
services, constitutes the main regionally mobile sector of the
economy as a whole. It also is crucial to the promotion of
local jobs and incomes in services. If you bring 100 manufacturing jobs into a problem area they will by themselves
generate an additional 80 jobs in local services over a period
of from three to five years. But the manufacturing must be
provided in the first place. Government intervention to
provide 80 jobs in services will not automatically pull in the
100 jobs in manufacturing.[27]

It has already been seen that previous regional grants and
incentives — on the firms' own evidence — did not bite either
sufficiently or at all on the leading manufacturing companies
which are most capable of organising a major initiative in a
new area, and or surviving there once established through their
overall market power. The reason lies not in any significant
location costs in UK problem regions and areas, but in the
massively greater gain which such companies can make by
going multinational rather than multiregional.[28]

In other words, those multi-plant companies in modern
manufacturing which are most needed to equalise employment
opportunities between British regions are those which our
present incentives least attract to those regions. The same is
true of the previously powerful location control in the form
of IDCs or Industrial Development Certificates. Where companies are national rather than multinational, IDCs can bite
hard. They can even prove damaging to the expansion prospects
of medium and small firms which lack the professional division
of management capable of coordinating either a successful new
venture or its management several hundred miles from the home
plant. This management factor is much more important than
the negligible increase in transport costs from net distance and
can in some cases act as a disincentive to expansion itself. But
for multinational companies IDCs are hardly a barrier at all.
They can be holed virtually at will by threatening to locate the
new venture abroad if the company is not allowed an IDC
exemption and permitted to expand near the major metropoli-

tan areas or recreation centres of the South and South East,
which senior management normally prefers when labour is
available in order to give middle management compensation
for a stint in less developed countries, or to make easier a part
time job or Bond Street shopping by the manager's wife. In
evidence to the Commons Expenditure Committee Unilever
cited this factor of suiting the middle manager's wife as the
most important in regional location in Britain. IBM also
frankly admitted that they secured IDC exemption to expand
at Havant because they told the government that otherwise
they would go abroad.[29]

Even if there were no other case for the public ownership
of leading manufacturing companies, only ownership could
right this gross imbalance between public and private power
in regional development. Under the prevailing legal and institutional structure, only ownership will bring control over the
management of such companies, and make it possible to close
the gulf which has emerged between their private interest and
that of the public at large.

One of the remarkable features of Italian public holdings
from the later sixties lies in their achievement of so much with
a relatively small base, in regional development. The IRI State
Holding has performed *ten times better than the private sector*
in placing jobs in the South of Italy — the main national, regional
problem. From 1968 to 1972 it created 60 per cent of new manufacturing jobs in the region, yet did so with control of only 6
per cent of total national manufacturing employment, during
a period of recession caused by a crisis in *private* sector investment from 1968 onwards.[30] It can be seen how much better a
really substantial British public sector in manufacturing could
perform in both national and regional development. Under
strategic government control, it could plan through the private
sector trade cycle and iron out the go-stop which has dogged
the British economy since the war. It also could modernise
and rationalise existing industrial structures without the fear-
some social costs which at present accompany such rationalisation when it occurs (as in the GEC-AEI merger), or may
in future be recommended (as in British Leyland).

CHAPTER EIGHT

Countervailing Multinationals

New public enterprise is new not only in the sense of allowing the government in the public interest to harness the market power of big league firms. It also is new in the sense that it can undertake jobs which the private leaders either will not do well, do reluctantly and at high public cost through subsidy, or fail to do at all while still taking the public's money through indirect and direct State aid.

In other words, while new public enterprise at the level of leading firms shares features with first generation nationalisation, its focus in firms in profitable sectors gives it genuinely new potential for promoting the public interest. Nationalisation as it has occurred through much of the capitalist world has taken over what is already there and put it into shape. New public enterprise both can take over what is already there, and from this base create something new. Starting from public holdings in existing enterprises, it can pioneer new roles close to the technical frontier of the economy. If coordinated and socially controlled, it also can overcome the main differences between private versus social costs under a predominantly private enterprise system. It can transform the social inefficiency of the private firm sector into social effectiveness in the public's real interest.

This becomes clear in the direct and indirect leverage which competitive public enterprise can give to a government in countervailing multinational capital. Various interrelated elements in the multinational challenge to economic sovereignty have already been outlined. They include the undermining of fiscal and monetary policy; the partial eclipse of exchange rate changes as an instrument of trade policy; exchequer loss, balance of payments cost and inflationary pressure from transfer pricing, and the blackmail of multinational location if they are not allowed the regional location in Britain of their choice.

The main respect in which public enterprise of leading firms can countervail multinational companies lies in the capacity of such public enterprise to *directly* undertake the jobs which tax concessions and cash handouts to private enterprise fail to promote.

In other words, by moving the focus of economic policy to big league firms in the directly productive meso-economic sector, the government can translate interest rate changes and tax changes at the macro-demand level to the leading enterprise and major projects whose activity now has a major effect on macro-economic outcomes.

The nationalisation of British Leyland could illustrate and pioneer the new case. Despite a declining market share, the company is still the major exporter of motor vehicles in the country. What it needs is public money under public ownership to substitute for the failure of the stock market to provide risk capital. It needs this to modernise through expanding its strong market areas and introducing entirely new product ranges. It also needs such public ownership and capital to equalise the now unequal terms of competition with the foreign private producers in the UK, which are more multi-national in operation and therefore secure the wider range of benefits on specialisation, access to Euro-market finance, and multinational scheduling of debt and payments which is not open on the same scale to the largely national British Leyland company. Through British Leyland as a public enterprise company, the government would not have to lower the macro-economic interest rate or tax on motor vehicles in the hope that the firm would respond with a raised rate of investment and rationalisation. British Leyland's problem is internal to the company as well as external in the unequal competition sense just outlined. Its resolution lies in new entrepreneurship in which the decision to modernise must come first, with the finance then made available, rather than the much less certain reverse sequence, where money has been made available, but the company had not modernised.

But these are still indirect forms of leverage on private multi-nationals made possible through the extension of a genuine public-private mix in the big league firms. There also are direct means for promoting such main aims of government economic strategy through the competitive public enterprise itself.

In prices, this can take the form of lower rates of increase or temporary reduction nearer to cost in main lines of activity. In general this will be possible to the extent that private sector multinationals are reaping super-normal profits relative to the micro-economic or small firm sector. Where such high prices have taken place through the self-charging of high imports from foreign subsidiaries, such import charges could be lowered and make possible the restraint of domestic price increases, subject to the needs of some of the less developed countries in which foreign subsidiaries would be located. In most cases, this form of price restraint would have leadership effects on other firms in the industry, which would be forced to follow the public sector leaders in restraining prices or lose market share to them. In some cases, such price restraint would cause problems for the less efficient small and medium sized firms in the industry which have hitherto sheltered under the 'price umbrella' of the leaders. However, such problems would be secondary and relatively small scale. This is because of the dualistic market structures which have evolved in what nominally are the same industry, and where the smaller enterprises serve mainly local markets which it is not in the interest of the big league to mop up. Otherwise, a regionalised agency or agencies could ensure either that the small firms were modernised and regrouped in more efficient units, or that their labour force was absorbed by the expansion of output and jobs initiated by public enterprise in the big league sector.

Such a price restraint policy through public sector leadership would tackle at source the previous perversity of price-making power by the private big league leaders. *If* the new public enterprise is sufficiently wide-ranging, its counter-inflation effects could have a positive feed-back on wages. Lower prices would mean higher real wages. Through restraining the rate of inflation both in the big league firms and in those other firms which bought from or were led by them, public enterprise

price restraint therefore could serve to reduce the pressure of
those wage demands which represent the just concern of working
people to protect their real wage levels in a period of major
inflation.

To the extent that public sector price restraint in manufacturing industry represented the reduction of inflated imports
from foreign subsidiaries it would directly contribute to import
saving in the best sense. I.e., it would reduce the exchange value
of the imported goods and their impact on the visible trade
account without reducing the use value of the imports themselves. But public enterprise ranged through the meso-economic
sector in manufacturing could also contribute directly to the
reduction of imports and export promotion. By definition,
any production of goods for sale on the home market reduces
imports if it is assumed that the goods otherwise would have
been purchased from abroad. But whereas such a process now
largely occurs through decisions based on their own world
wide interests by multinational companies in the private,
sector, planning through leading public enterprise could ensure that investment capacity in entirely new plant in this
country was raised to a level in which it both could substitute
for imports and also leave a margin for export promotion
abroad.

In practice, there are important links between scale of investment, embodied technology, lowered prices and improvement in the balance of trade. Larger scale 'offensive' investment in entirely new plant can raise productivity much higher
than small scale investment of the 'defensive' or incremental
type. This process arises mainly through the greater chance to
maximise design efficiency of equipment and plant layout,
plus fuller use of higher productivity equipment at critical
parts of the production process. This can permit lower prices
reflecting lower real costs. If the strategic features of the
public firm's foreign trade are planned with unions and the
government on the lines of the Planning Agreements system,
this can ensure that the maximum direct promotion of exports and domestic import substitution is ensured through
such offensive public sector investment. None of this
should be surprising. Britain at present has some of the

most capable and internally efficient leading companies in Europe. What the country notoriously lacks is the high growth which is technically feasible if enough leading companies simultaneously expand investment and orders from other companies. The planning of such linkages between leading firms in a coordinated expansion, focussed on price restraint and an improved trade position lies in our grasp if sufficient public enterprise ranging through manufacturing industry can be directly harnessed to the broad wave of investment we need. However, we can only escape the vicious circle of the go-stop syndrome and enjoy the benefits of 'virtuous circle' expansion if public enterprise in big league firms ranges through manufacturing industry as a whole. Otherwise some industry cylinders will fire, others will not, and the economy will continue to stagger from go to stop or lose momentum over the long run.

But what about private sector multinational blackmail, either in individual cases on location, or more generally in the form of the threat to close down in this country or locate all further expansion abroad?

In the first place, this is likely only for some multinationals rather than all big league companies. The multinationals are already facing the possibility of public sector takeover in other European countries and less developed countries round the world. The programmes of the parties of the French and Italian Left are increasingly converging both domestically (between parties) and with Labour's 1973 Programme. The new convergence shows a readiness of mass labour movements and socialist parties in opposition to frame strategies for countervailing multinational capital through selective public ownership. In addition one of the main strengths of the international trades union movement lies not only in its power to contest the action of an individual multinational company but also in its collective strength to pressure the foreign subsidiaries of a group of multinationals in the event of their directly challenging the economic sovereignty of a democratically elected socialist government in another country. In other words, firm political and industrial action *can* counteract multinational blackmail *if* governments of the Left act to implement their own policies decisively with international union support.

Secondly, any socialist government in Britain would be foolhardy to spearhead its new public sector in manufacturing industry through takeover or attempted takeover of foreign based and controlled multinationals. It has enough British owned multinationals in the big league from which to choose a broad base of multinational public enterprise in manufacturing. Through securing control of such British based multinationals it would thereby gain controlling shareholdings in their subsidiaries abroad. Any maverick British board attempting a last ditch fight for private monopoly power might find an ally in South Africa, but would not be supported in most of the Western economies in which the new publicly controlled multinational would operate unless their governments chose to contest the decision of the British government, and hazard a wide range of international issues on which cooperation is needed in the present economic crisis. In less developed countries, governments might well press for a joint shareholding in the subsidiaries of the new public sector multinationals. But such a policy should be both acceptable to and welcomed by any government in a developed country which is paying more than lip service to Third World development.

Thirdly, it is not true that a major nation state cannot effectively bring part of a multinational company into public ownership through lack of the wide range of subsidiaries into which that part is integrated round the world. This depends on the range of the new public sector available to the government, and the manner and time horizon in which it plans for a diversification of that sector in the public interest. As the Italians clearly showed when the Raytheon electronics company pulled out of a venture in Southern Italy, diverisified State Holding Company can integrate the existing plant and facilities into a new long term programme for the sector. This was particularly graphic in the Italian case, where the State Holdings were not already represented on more than a token scale in electronics. In conjunction with the government they built up a ten year national programme for electronics based on bringing the Raytheon company's plant and facilities into a new State electronics company. This is in process of completing the creation of 30,000 new jobs in electronics, selling in part to the rest of the public sector, located exclusively in the problem region of Southern Italy.[31]

In practice the Italians have already found that this capacity to absorb, diversify and expand the plant and facilities of a private multinational company has acted as a deterrent to abuse multinational power by leading firms in the meso-economic sector. For example, in the late 1960's three leading Italian companies in the food processing industry were threatened with takeover by two US multinational companies. The government learned from them that they planned to import foreign agricultural produce, process it in Northern Italy and sell mainly on the domestic market. This would have reduced the possibility of focussing the expansion of these industries in the problem region of the South and would have damaged the balance of payments through increasing imports and decreasing exports. After consulting the IRI State Holding Company, the government secured assurances that the expansion of processing through manufacture was viable in the South, using southern agricultural produce, and focussing sales on exports. It therefore gave IRI the go ahead to take a controlling shareholding in the Italian companies concerned — Alemagna, Motta and Cirio — and safeguard the enterprises under public ownership in a planning framework.

CHAPTER NINE

Size and Selection

The previous analysis shows that new public enterprise can fulfil the main economic roles outlined in Labour's Programme 1973 provided it is represented in leading companies over a sufficiently broad range of manufacturing industry. But how should one choose such firms in the first place, and what would be the critical minimum size necessary to ensure that the such interrelated gains from new public enterprise can be secured?

It is no accident that this became a contentious issue in the drafting of Labour's Programme 1973, most notably in the claim of the Opposition Green Paper on the National Enterprise Board (Labour's State Holding) which stated that "dependent on their size, the takeover of some twenty to twenty five companies" from the top hundred manufacturers would be essential over a five year term "if the public sector is to exercise an effective role in economic planning". The Green Paper also argued that such a range of new public enterprise should ultimately control a third of the turnover, two fifths of the profits and about half of the employment of the top hundred manufacturing companies. Broadly speaking, since the top hundred at that time controlled about half of manufacturing, these figures could be divided in half for a rough indication of total manufacturing share, i.e. about a sixth of turnover a fifth of profits and a quarter of employment in manufacturing as a whole.

This was quantification of the case for fundamentally reversing the dominance of private power in this sector of big league firms. It was the case for public enterprise command of the new heights of big league manufacturing.

It was clear that the figure of companies actually given —

from twenty to twenty five was neither '25' nor the top '25' rather than twenty to twenty five from the top hundred firms in the meso-economic sector. Such number games give interesting results in terms of Mr. Roy Jenkins' earlier proposal for a major State Holding Company as an instrument of national and regional development. Like the NEC proposals, this has a base in Rolls-Royce, BP, ICL and a couple of other companies in which the government already had a holding, plus a recommended expansion into ten other specified industries. On minimum arithmetic this gives a Jenkins Holding of 15 companies versus 20 to 25 in the NEC proposal.[32]

There was a strong case for publishing the names of companies which would fit the bill in terms of the criteria for new public ownership outlined in the Green Paper and in Labour's Programme. The French Socialist and Communist Parties did so in their Common Programme for Government, and this did not prevent François Mitterand from coming within one per cent of the vote sufficient for him to make him President of the Republic and form a government of the United Left. In other words, the naming of big league firms for public ownership was part of a campaign which yielded better results than any previously conducted by the social democratic Left in France.

In practice, a Labour government determined to extend public enterprise through the big league sector will be likely to find candidate companies dropping in its lap through inflation, a parasitic stock market which now finances less than 2 per cent of the investment in British manufacturing industry, and inefficient management which claims up to the time of private bankruptcy that public enterprise will ruin the country.

However, a Labour government should use its own policy guide lines for selective public ownership of manufacturing companies if it is seriously in the business of harnessing the power of the big private companies in the public interest. The economic criteria as established in Labour's Programme 1973 and the two election manifestos of 1974 include:

(1)   job creation, especially in areas of high unemployment;

    (2) investment promotion;
    (3) technological development;
    (4) growth of exports;
    (5) import substitution;
    (6) promoting government price policies and tackling
          the spread of multinational companies.

These criteria were re-iterated in the August 1974 government White Paper *The Regeneration of British Industry*, and
partly reflected in the government's Industry Bill of January
1975.

Anyone will realise that not all of the criteria are quanti-
fiable. Qualitative judgements have to be made. For instance,
interpretation of the export capacity of a firm or its ability
to counteract a foreign based multinational demand an
assessment of the management competence and operating
capacity of the firm over time. Also, sheer quantitive size
may not be the most important factor in determining the
suitability of a big league firm to pioneer such role. The number
one company today may well be a potential lame duck of the
first order. By contrast, a cygnet company number five or six
in its own league stakes may well be the best potential swan
in the business. It may already have grown fast with a well coordinated management team but now face obstacles to further
expansion. These could include 'no entry' barriers imposed by
other big league firms at home or foreign multinationals block-
ing its access to the overseas markets necessary to cover the
costs of a large investment project of the 'enterprise' or 'offensive' investment type. Alternatively, it could face uncertainty about the long term expansion of demand from its principal
client companies on the home market, uncertainty about
what it would be allowed under the go-stop cycle of government prices policy, further uncertainty whether it would be
allowed to take over a competitor as the base for further challenge to the leaders in its sector under a prevailing liberal
capitalist ideology in the Monopolies Commission, and so on.

In all these areas, public ownership could help management
in such a company — whether conventional or workers' controlled — to fulfil its expansionary objectives. Barriers imposed

by larger companies at home or abroad depend on the bigger firm's greater access to finance to ride out the competitive challenge by temporarily holding prices stable, or lowering them for the kill of the would-be entrant. Only a glutton for punishment in either the national or multinational league would play this game when the backer of the expanding public sector firm was the government itself. It would lose cash flow and probably find itself in anti-monopoly action supervised by the company's sponsor department. Precisely because the company was a public rather than a private sector challenger, the monopolistic entry barriers either would not be lowered, or if they already had been, would tend to be lifted.

Probably the leading company *would* choose to restrain its future rate of price increase, but for competitive reasons over the long term rather than short-term difficulties which normally hit a smaller challenger in the entry stakes, with private financial institutions withholding support from it precisely because they know that the struggle for survival is unequal. With clear government backing over the investment horizon of a competitive project, the smaller firm could both survive and grow, producing at lower real cost per unit of output i.e. higher productivity, making it possible to sell at lower prices in line with the larger company which had been compelled to follow its lead.

While public ownership could help such an intermediate firm in the big league sector to expand decisively despite initially unequal competition, so pre-agreement between the government and the enterprise on a specific price level for the product over the medium term, or agreement to a strategic merger could enable it to break from a defensive to an offensive market posture against the topmost firms, increasing the area in which expanded jobs, increased wages and lowered priced benefited both the labour force and the industrial or personal consumer.

In other words, the actual selection of such a company should be influenced by quantitative data on performance, but also would involve a qualitative judgement on the company and a politicised process of negotiation with its management.

In other cases the quantitative data on market share, trade and pricing over time could indicate clear monopoly abuse and a classic monopoly case for outright public ownership. If this were contested by some of the management, the opponents of public ownership could test the open labour market they applaud from the board and put their talents up for hire elsewhere.

These are combined quantitative and qualitative factors of the kind that any merchant bank would exercise as a matter of routine when employed to assess the virtue of a merger or takeover. There is nothing especially new in such a process except the principle that the government should get in on the deal and use the market power of the company for the public welfare rather than the entrenchment of private meso-economic power.

But in purely quantitative terms there is preliminary work which the government can undertake as the rolling framework within which such judgements could be made on company selection for public ownership. This can be operated at both the inter-industry and intra-industry level, and serviced by information collated through the Planning Agreements system described in the following chapter.

For instance, the French planners have consciously used trade statistics against the performance of individual leader firms in the meso-economic sector. In other words, they have first identified sectors of high import dependence or sectors in which there is a notable export bottleneck. They then have got hold of firms A and B and prompted them through their combination of consultant, banker and plain bully to get on with import substitution or export promotion.[33] There were specific reasons why this process worked well enough in France in the postwar period of high and sustained economic growth, when there were fewer big league giants and virtually no multinationals. State power over private enterprise was then very considerable, and a wide range of public enterprise was not a *necessary* condition for relatively effective planning. Nonetheless, the same principles can be applied to the selection of potential new public enterprises for the push role in exports or the restraint of imports in individual sectors. The quanti-

tative data by firm and industry will delineate the main area
of choice, with a handful of firms capable of exercising any
considerable effect in individual sectors.

What holds for quantitative background data on trade also holds
for the other main areas of investment, technology, prices and
regional development. A clear sign of under-investment is available
from those firms in the big league sector which are lagging in terms
of the proportion of internally retained funds allocated to re-invest-
ment. A preliminary sign of technical progress comes from the
proportion of own company funds allocated to research and development. According to Belgian planners this method is practicable
as a guideline, despite the fact that many multinationals choose
to use this holdall item of expenditure as a cover for taking funds
out of the country. In prices, the average percentage rate of increase for selected items in the company's range can be broken
down over time to identify who leads when, and how often, with
particular price increases. It was through analysis of such timing in
price leadership that a local generating company in the United
States identified the more problematic phenomenon of collusive
pricing in the US electrical switchgear market which ultimately
led to gaol sentences on several boardroom worthies from Westing-
house, General Electric and other leaders in the US meso-economic
sector.[34] Also, systematic deficits on imports traded into this
country from foreign subsidiaries are a *prima facie* sign of transfer
pricing.

In regional development potential, the criteria are simpler.
Heavily capital intensive industries are excellent. Figures on the
range of labour intensity by industry are already available, ranging
from a factor of 25 in steel to 8 in electronics, 4 in shoes, and 3
in clothing. Also, within such relatively labour intensive industries,
as already shown from the meso-economic and micro-economic
firms tend to demonstrate measurably different degrees of loca-
tional mobility.

On such quantitive data alone, serviced by appropriate com-
puting calculating equipment and a handful of qualified staff, the
seven economic criteria in Labour's Programme could be run off
in an inter-industry and intra-industry analysis sufficient to rank
companies or most of the criteria through manufacturing industry.

CHAPTER TEN

The Planning Agreements System

A major new instrument of economic planning has already
been outlined in Labour's Programme 1973 and the 1974
election manifestoes. This is the Planning Agreements
system aimed at transforming big business power.

It has been stressed that the expansion of the existing
public sector and a new mix in the economy will be a necessary condition for the success of this system in the private
sector. Without such new public enterprise ranging through
the main private sectors in industry the agreements system
either will not work, or will only work ineffectively. This is
most important in the manufacturing heartland of the economy.

But it also is essential for the success of the Planning Agreements system that it should apply to both major firms in the
private sector and to public enterprise. This should include not
only the new public enterprises brought into the NEB
but also the existing single sector nationalised industries and
services such as the Steel Corporation, Coal Board, British
Rail, Post Office etc. The guideline for those private and
public enterprises brought into the system would in the first
instance be the Category 1 benchmark in the Tory government's Counter-Inflation bill — i.e. £50 millions turnover or
more a year at 1973 prices.[35]

As summarised in Labour's Programme 1973, the role of
the Planning Agreements system includes:

— Securing up to date information, on a systematic and
continuing basis, from *all* companies and enterprises within the
system *and certainly the top 100 manufacturing companies.*

This information will concern both past performance and
advance programmes — programmes which can be checked
at a later date against results. It will cover such areas as:

(1)   investment and its location,
(2)   prices,
(3)   product development,
(4)   marketing,
(5)   exports,
(6)   import requirements.

(These six criteria *parallel* the main areas in which it is intended
that the National Enterprise Board should intervene in the
economy.)

— Using this information to help the Labour government
to identify and achieve its planning objectives and to plan
for the redistribution of resources which will be needed to
meet those objectives.

— Securing the agreement of the firms and enterprises
within the system — the written Planning Agreement — that
they will help the government to meet certain clearly defined
objectives)e.g. a certain number of new jobs in a Development Area) — while leaving the tactics which will be needed
to achieve these strategic objectives to the companies and
enterprises.

— Providing for the regular revision of the Agreements in
the light of experience and progress.

— Providing a basis for channelling selective government
assistance directly to those firms which agree to help us meet
the nation's planning objectives.

— Providing a systematic basis for making large companies and enterprises accountable for their behaviour, and
for bringing into line those which refuse to cooperate — using
where necessary both the extensive powers under our proposed Industry Act, the activities of our new and existing
public enterprises, and the powers of public purchasing.

— Publishing a detailed annual report to the nation on the

record of the companies and enterprises in the system, and on
their progress — or lack of it — in meeting the nation's economic objectives."[36]

Potentially, such wide ranging planning through the dominant firms in the economy gives us the chance to transform
private dominance *if* we use Planning Agreements as the
counterpart of new public ownership and new industrial democracy through union bargaining of the agreements themselves.

The Planning Agreements system should *not* mean that
company management — whether conventional or worker
self-managed — would be told what to do by civil servants
with little or no experience of industry. The government
nonetheless must use the system decisively — backed by its
new public enterprise and by the powers under the Industry
Act — as a primary means of ensuring a shift from private
domination of the commanding heights of the economy to a
dominance of public accountability and control.

The possibility of such a combination of greater public
power with a wide degree of continued freedom for enterprise
lies in the distinction between *strategy* and *tactics*. Basically,
the government will be intervening in the activities of strategic firms in strategic industries. These are both the new meso-
economic firms in the key industries and services on which
the viability of the British economy and the very feasibility
of government economic management itself depends.

But the government should not itself be drawing up the
programme of the companies and corporations which will be
scrutinised under the Planning Agreements system. For both
the existing and new public sectors, plus the other firms
brought into the system, enterprise would be left free to
initiate its own programmes. The government would then
determine whether or not these programmes conform with
its strategic economic objectives. These are issues concerning the kind of information made available to it through
the Planning Agreements, i.e. investment, job location, prices,
product development, marketing, exports, and imports.

In many cases the programmes of the public and private
sector could be cleared with little or no modification. This

will be most likely in those cases where the enterprises themselves have initially taken account of the government's overall economic and social objectives. In other cases, the government could make plain it considers that either a public or private enterprise is failing the nation through insufficient expansion of investment, jobs or exports, inadequate provision for the location of new jobs in areas of employment decline, excessive advertising expenditure or deceptive consumer promotion at the cost of the public, and so on.

In practice the Planning Agreements system need not substitute imperative government planning for the indicative planning of the National Plan, or the indicative targeting of budget statements traditionally made by Chancellors of the Exchequer. But it should be *more* than indicative while *less* than wholly imperative. Tactical selectivity is possible when there is a strategic policy for industry based on the reversal of private criteria and private dominance.

Thus the government should employ imperative powers where necessary, and these powers can advance considerably on the purely indicative planning of the National Plan. But in the first instance the Planning Agreements process could be indicative. The enterprises would show to the government what they intend to do in the light of overall economic objectives, and the government in return would indicate where it considers that divergences of public interest and private enterprise arise.

In general, therefore the Planning Agreements system should operate as a *systematised bargaining process* between the government and the giant private and public corporations which have become so important to the national economy. Government pressure on private enterprise leaders could take the form of requiring the firm to bring forward the introduction of an investment or modernisation programme which the firm itself had scheduled for a later date; increasing the volume of a particular export project, or rationalising projected additions to capacity in existing plant through an entirely new plant located in a problem region or area. Such pressure exercised in an ad hoc or once off manner would discriminate against one firm rather than others and on occasion could lead to economic costs. But the increased size and market power of the new big league firms means that coordinated pressure on as few as twenty to thirty enterprises during a given year could have a significant effect on counter-cyclical policy, the visible trade balance, and regional employment.

Where necessary, the government's leverage — or the more imperative element in new economic planning — could operate in three main ways anticipated in Labour's Programme 1973:

(1)   the sanction that new public enterprises represented in the industry would be used to fulfil a planning objective if this was resisted by a private enterprise leader;

(2)   the withholding of government financial assistance, and the re-negotiation of such assistance, through the new system, on the basis of revealed need, plus

(3)   the public or Social Audit of the main features of the Planning Agreements reached between the government and the enterprises — i.e. publication of the main part of the Planning Agreement.

It has already been argued that new public enterprise ranging through the Category 1 area of the economy — the meso-sector — is essential to secure not only the sanction that a public enterprise will act where private leaders hesitate, but also to secure information on the real nature of cost and profit schedules in the industry. It also has been shown that evidence from leading companies on the minimal significance of major regional grants and incentives reveals that present aids and incentives to the private sector leaders are massively in excess of need and a squandering of public money in the private sector. In general the leading private sector firms should be required to reach deep into the kind of funds which they have been syphoning abroad through transfer pricing in meeting their future investment needs. If they then threaten to locate abroad where other governments still subsidize them despite their enormous private resources, a socialist government should not hesitate to bring them into public ownership.

This should be the new name of the game in the interface between the public and private sectors under Labour's planning system. If confrontation is called, it will be called by some of the wealthiest companies in the world which, on their own evidence, either do not need or actually make a surplus from public assistance to the private sector. The Planning Agreements system cannot be used in any other way if a socialist government is to be master rather than servant of the new giant enterprises.

The Social Audit of the published Planning Agreements would in itself vastly democratise the process of strategic decision-making in the economy. When the government has decided to impose particular features of a Planning Agreement on an enterprise, it could publish the reasons for its decision in the Social Audit. The Audit could particularly stress the consumer implications of the enterprise's activity, including the past overall record on consumer pricing, terms of sale, advertising expenditure identified as a proportion of the cost of itemised household products, deterioration or improvement in the quality of public service, misleading or deceptive advertising, success or failure in meeting complaints on imperfect goods and service, and so on.

In drafting its Social Audit for the enterprises in the Planning Agreements system, the government could request written submissions from the re-introduced National Consumer Council, and from the respective consumer councils for the nationalised industries and services. It should make public those areas in which it has been influenced in its Planning Agreement with the enterprises by the evidence produced and argued by the respective councils, and should publish dissenting reports by the councils in those areas where they consider that government action has been insufficient to respond to consumer pressures.

This exercise would entail a considerable extension of the previous powers of the consumer councils, and constitute a major means of replacing producer sovereignty by a sovereignty for the public as consumer. But in order to make it effective the government would have to increase the funds and staffing of the central Consumer Council and open local branches of the Council, possibly with offices in Local Government establishments. This would give alternative access for complaints concerning the existing public sector, and permit the government to cross check and evaluate the nature of complaints through the new procedures.

The Social Audit through the published Planning Agreements also would represent a major advance on the present uncertainties concerning the advance planning of major companies. This should be available to those who work in these companies, and in those firms and enterprises dependent upon them for their own sales and jobs.

CHAPTER ELEVEN

Planning and Industrial Democracy

The Labour Party's February 1974 election manifesto wrote of "socialising the public sector". As it put it, "we intend to socialise existing nationalised industries in consultation with the unions. We shall take steps to make the management of existing nationalised industries more responsive to the workers in the industry . . . " The Liberal Party also has argued for several years in favour of industrial democracy. The TUC Interim Report on Industrial Democracy of 1973 recommended a two tier structure for management boards in the public sector, with fifty per cent of the supervisory board — the supreme decision making body of the enterprise — appointed through union and TUC machinery.[37] In his address as Leader of the Party to the 1973 Conference, Harold Wilson also punctuated his heavy pounding of the Tories with frequent references to the industrial democracy which Labour would ensure in power.

How can industrial democracy prove compatible with the kind of planning already outlined, where the government reserves the right of control after bargaining with firms themselves on the strategic aspects of their activity? Surely workers' control means that workers themselves should determine the nature of investment, prices, location, contribution to foreign trade and so on, instead of private management or central government?

This is a debate which will increasingly be shaped by workers in leading companies. The problems of workers' control in Yugoslavia are well enough known. The general freedom of workers' controlled firms to determine the pattern of prices, trade and location has contributed to a rate of inflation higher than in many West European countries, a persistent trend to balance of payments deficit, and a regional problem which has

worsened during a period in which the Italians — through State
capitalist measures — have succeeded in reducing regional dis-
parities.

What Labour must achieve is a form of democratic planning
which avoids the extremes of Soviet type over-centralisation
and under-centralisation of the Yugoslav type or the anarchic
capitalist market. The key to resolving the dilemma between
central controls and local worker autonomy lies in the distinction between *strategy* and *tactics*. The distinction paral-
lels the strategy-tactics mechanism outlined for the Planning
Agreements system. By this system leading public and private
enterprises would be obliged to submit their corporate strategies to the government in advance for assessment of compati-
bility with the new planning objectives — investment and export expansion, new jobs in problem regions, etc.

This means bringing the management teams into government
and bargaining out the pros and cons of the companies' and the
government's case. The general initiative on strategy plus the
tactics by which they fulfilled an agreed strategic Planning
Agreement would be up to the companies themselves.

Workers in large private and public enterprises should be
given the option of taking part in this bargaining through the
Planning Agreements. This need not undermine traditional
bargaining procedures in the companies. If the unions are in
disagreement with the management (whether public or
private enterprise), they can come separately to Whitehall
and state their separate case.*

Through taking part in the negotiation of Planning Agreements, workers within companies will be able to take the issues
which affect them most directly from the shop floor to the
corridors and committee rooms in Whitehall where State
power has proverbially been concentrated.

This new dimension to industrial democracy is a crucial
safeguard against bi-lateral decision making between management and government affecting the conditions and livelihood
of millions of workers in the economy. Enlightened technocracy

---

*   Since the following argument was drafted in 1973, its main
     features have been embodied in the August 1974 government
     White Paper *The Regeneration of British Industry.*

can intervene in the planning of the economy in such a way as to promote some increases in welfare. But no such conspiracy in the public interest is either genuinely democratic or genuinely socialist. If the new forward planning through leading companies made possible through Planning Agreements is to promote a transformation of the society in which we live, it can only be through the consent of the majority of workers in those companies.

It should not be obligatory on workers in companies in the Planning Agreements to take part in agreements. No legislation should oblige them, nor a uniform formula be recommended by which they might take part. The main aim of this new dimension to democratic planning should be to open the door to workers to take part in the negotiation with government and management of the main features of their companies' programmes over the medium term. It can be anticipated that workers nonetheless would wish to take part in such negotiation on a wide scale, and that they would choose to do so through representation organised within their traditional trades union structures, operating through combine committees in the companies brought into the system.

The potential gains for workers through taking part in the bargaining of Planning Agreements are open-ended. What they want to bargain, as well as how they do it, will be up to workers themselves.

The government should require management to make available to workers' representatives the information which they are submitting to the government for negotiation in the Planning Agreement. This should include:-

1. Projected investment and employment in the UK and abroad;
2. Specification of the regional implications of expansions to existing plant, proposed mergers and rationalisations;
3. Projected targets for the company's or corporation's international trade, with a separate breakdown of trade between the UK company and its multinational subsidiaries where the enterprise is multinational in operation;
4. A past breakdown and future projection of profits in-

cluding the relative shares of corporate income to wage
labour, amortisation and investment, management salaries
and share options, and distributed share income.

(The August 1974 White Paper *The Regeneration of
British Industry* proposed such revelation of information
to workers through joint union bargaining of Planning
Agreements. *Some* of this range of information has been
included in the January 1975 Industry Bill.)

Workers also should be invited to submit proposals for the
diversification and expansion of their companies, and to forward
such proposals in the context of a more socially directed expenditure and direction of resources than at present undertaken
by some management in the private sector. The structure of
this negotiation by workers of Planning Agreements is illustrated
in Figure 6, and the right hand column 4, Figure 7.

This should not mean that workers taking part in the bargaining of Planning Agreements would thereby forego the right to
forward proposals to the government for the public ownership
or social ownership of their enterprise under workers' control.

In order to ensure that such worker access to the bargaining
of Planning Agreements represents a genuinely new dimension
to industrial democracy, it is crucial that workers in big firms
should themselves elect representatives from the unions in their
own companies for such bargaining, rather than act through
their national union representatives or the TUC itself. Otherwise the negotiation would be too distant from the shopfloor
or office to involve working people directly, and overcome
the present psychology of the 'them versus us' syndrome.

Nonetheless, just as it could be expected that workers
would choose to organise their own representation through
union structures at the company level, it also could be expected that the union officials concerned would act in close
liaison with their national union officers and research depart-
ments, and through them with the TUC in cases of important
national interest. In other words, the new procedure made
possible through inviting workers' representatives to take
part from the start in Planning Agreements would represent a
supplement to traditional union bargaining rather than substitute for it. This is illustrated in the context of the overall

framework for the bargaining of the Social Contract in between the TUC and the Cabinet — in Figure 7.

The organisation of workers' representation at company level would be a major exercise, posing major challenges to workers' organisation in the giant companies which head the league in the Planning Agreements category. Some of the companies employ over 100,000 people in the private sector, and more in the public sector. In many cases leading private companies are themselves holding companies for a wide range of subsidiary enterprises of considerable size. There would be a strong case in such diversified or conglomerate companies for a separate negotiation on Planning Agreements and separate bargaining with government and management on the form which corporate planning should take. It also can be anticipated that cases of conflict of interests would arise between subsidiary companies in the same group. Nonetheless, in general the government should welcome the joint negotiation of Planning Agreements by workers' representatives acting on behalf of all companies within a group.

The issue of corporate secrecy in defence of legitimate business and commercial interest will be raised by some companies as an obstacle to the joint bargaining on Planning Agreements with workers' representatives.

In some cases a degree of secrecy will be necessary. On the other hand, most of the information negotiated through Planning Agreements need not contain so specific a breakdown as to reveal the particular market profile of a product, the design features it will incorporate, or the formula it embodies. As previously stressed, the government for its part will be concerned with the strategic features of company planning in enterprise of strategic importance to the national economy. In many cases it will be dealing with global figures even when these are broken into specific product, investment or profit categories.

Much hot air will be ventilated on this issue as an excuse by big business for inaction. But any government keeping its cool will stress the real issues and press on with the revelation.

The Planning Agreements system should emphasise the unleashing of talent and ability rather than its restraint.

We are not starting from a golden age or Garden of Eden in
which either management or unions are free to act without
responsibility to the community as a whole. The break-
through in initiative and socially controlled enterprise made
possible through a tri-partite structure for the negotiation
of Planning Agreements lies in the advance bargaining which it
will permit between the government, management in leading
public and private enterprise, and workers in the enterprise
concerned. It will not mean a formula for the automatic avoid-
ance of conflict. But it will mean a formula in which conflict
in many cases can be more clearly defined and more feasibly
resolved in the interests of working people as a whole.

Such a democratised negotiation of corporate planning would
permit a new dimension to workers' control in the sense that
workers negotiated corporate strategy either independently
from conventional management or through their own workers'
appointed management (with a supervisory role in the government department where the agreement was negotiated). Both
roles would genuinely extend the range of worker control from
the shop floor to Whitehall.

But there are other virtues from the introduction of new
strategic planning on the lines sketched in previous chapters.
Provided the enormous power of big companies in the system
— the meso-economic leaders — is harnessed and coordinated
in the public interest, the smaller enterprises in the micro-
economic sector can be subjected to *less* government intervention than planned by the Tories under Stage 3 of their so-called
counter-inflation policy. In simple terms, the companies in the
top hundred category have a greater impact on the outcome
of macro-economic aggregates than the companies in the category from one hundred to eight hundred (Category 2 in the
Tories' Counter-Inflation Policy). For the thousands of
smaller enterprises which crowd into the remaining micro-
economic sector a major initiative in innovation or exports can
be important, but it is much less important in terms of its
impact on the national economy than in the big meso-economic
league. As illustrated in Figure 6, many smaller firms are at
present lagging behind the industry leaders, and desperately
in need of the new initiative which majority workers'

control could release.

There is a simple justice in such division of powers between government and workers in big and small companies (the meso- and micro-economic league). It is crucial that the corporate planning of the meso-economic leaders should serve the wider interests of society through a coordinated framework if we are to advance on the failure of the National Plan and the disappointments of Yugoslav type decentralisation. From one viewpoint this qualifies the total freedom of workers in giant companies to choose precisely what they produce, at what price, with what contribution to foreign trade, and so on. On the other hand, of course, it widens the voice of workers in these companies in the process of democratic planning of the national social and economic strategy. Worker controlled companies in the micro-economic sector will be more free to determine precisely what they produce, the prices at which they sell, and so on, though they inversely have less chance to contribute directly to the bargaining of national social and economic strategy through the Planning Agreements system.

Such simple justice could be sophisticated if extended bargaining between national unions and the government were forwarded as an intrinsic part of the social contract. In other words, members of national unions in small companies in the micro-economic sector would still have a strong voice in the direct overall bargaining between the TUC and the government on the overall economic and social strategy of the country.

In other words, while the workers in leading companies in the private meso-sector, and in the public corporations, would have some advantage over micro-economic firms in being able to bargain directly on issues affecting national economic strategy, they should be expected to trade-off their personal gains against the gains to other workers (frequently in the same unions) in smaller firms in the economy. These smaller firms often would be located in problem regions and areas which desperately need new investment and jobs which could be brought in through new plant where location was bargained through the Planning Agreements system.

As illustrated in Figure 7, the regional executives of the unions could negotiate directly with the joint unions of

leading companies, and in cases of difference of opinion refer
the matter to national union level or to the TUC itself. As
with the Cabinet in relation to differences of opinion between
ministers, the TUC in major and exceptional cases could be
the ultimate arbiter of inter-union differences arising at regional
or executive level.

CHAPTER TWELVE

Socialism and the Social Contract

The main socialist dimensions of Labour's strategy should now be clear. They include not only a penetration of the commanding heights of modern capitalism in the meso-economic sector, but also the simultaneous transformation of the prevailing class structures which concentrate economic and social power in the hands of a self-perpetuating oligarchy. This can never be a complete or final process. There is no socialist utopia at the end of a specific programme for transformation. There is no socialist 'new man' waiting to spring from the beach-head of the social frontier. We cannot be expected to arise as from a sermon on the mount and love our neighbours as un-dividedly as we love ourselves.

On the other hand, we do not have to fall victim to capitalist mythology and believe that individual fulfilment lies exclusively in the pursuit of self-interest. There is already extensive evidence for this not only in the altruistic tradition of progressive Chris-tianity over two thousand years, but also in the extent to which a high proportion of the educated young now choose to follow careers which involve social service, under frustrating conditions, at real cost in relation to what they could earn in capitalist business. In most cases such people, young and old, represent a microcosm of socialist motivation. They do not work to deny themselves, but find such social service a fuller form of self-expression than the narrow self-interest of progress through a capitalist hierarchy.

In practice only a socialist party, representing a mass move-ment, can transform such motivation and such behaviour from the exception to the rule. In these terms socialism is the trans-lation of such a microcosm to the macrocosmic level, with transition spearheaded through new public ownership and social controls in the meso-economic sector. It is the creation of a society in which it is easier to secure self-fulfilment through serving society than through the exclusive pursuit of self alone. It is a society in which altruism is not self-denial, but the readiest form of self-expression. In political terms, it is a society in which people are both practical and idealists. It represents a system in which they can overcome their alienation from society and find their greatest fulfilment through working both in it at large and for it as a whole. It is not a theory, or an ideal world in which inter-personal or international differences are eliminated, but a system in which such differences occur within the maximum democracy feasible at all levels of society, and the maximum disposal of economic resources for the welfare of all the people. It is a society which will never be perfect in the eyes of all its members, but which will be transformed in relation to the gross imperfections and grotesque inequalities of contemporary capitalism.

Progress to socialism will be an on-going process, but one in which the critical centres of capitalist power and class can be confronted by a socialist government, backed by the trades unions. To transform modern capitalism, it will need to undertake what Tony Benn has called a fundamental change in the balance of power in favour of working people and their families.[38] It is crucial that such a change be achieved through democratic processes, and through reforms legislated in parliament. Without such democratic change, the challenge to capitalism may prove less a controlled transformation in the public interest, than a painful way of changing the form of power and exploitation in a still centralised and hierarchical society.

On the other hand, such democratic reforms must be effectively revolutionary in character. In other words, they must reverse the present dominance of capitalist modes of production and capitalist motivation into a dominance of democratically controlled socialism. They must transform capitalist society rather than try ineffectively to alleviate its inherent unefficiency and injustice.

To expect eighteen or twenty people round a cabinet table to initiate such change would be unrealistic unless they were backed by the economic and social force of the organised working class. It will only be through the negotiated and bargained support of the trades union movement that such critical change will prove to be possible. If it also is to be effective, such bargaining and such negotiation must involve a new dimension to the relationship between the Labour Party and the Labour movement, backed by new means for widening the effective control of working people over the main strategy for social and economic transformation. This means not only a social contract in the sense of agreement on the main strategy for transformation of capitalism, negotiated between government and the unions at the national level, but also a pioneering of means for working people either to control their own companies outright, or to take part in a process of national bargaining on the contribution which their firms should make both to themselves and to society as a whole. Such new dimensions to socialist planning are crucial if extended public enterprise and strategic planning are to promote transition to socialism rather than new dimensions to State capitalism, or State intervention in a bureaucratic structure and unreconstructed class framework.[39]

These wide reaching dimensions to the social contract are important and should be stressed. As originally conceived by Rousseau, the social contract amounted to pre-agreement on the way in which society would be run. In Rousseau's society, everyone would take part in the shaping of the initial contract with the legislator. It would aim to secure total agreement on the shape of society, subject to on-going revisions agreed with the legislator. It aimed *inter alia* to abolish the exploitation of a permanent minority by a permanent majority, and extend individual freedom rather than reduce it. It also aimed to abolish alienation of the individual's freedom through representative decision-making. In practice, Rousseau's contract was unrealisable in the large nation states of his time. Even those who drew on Rousseau during the French Revolution were forced to face the need for delegated decision making. Rousseau also wrote the Social Contract with the aim of preserving a pre-industrial society and in a pre-socialist context (though there are strong elements of egalitarianism in his writing).

In big companies, quite apart from big countries, the principle of representative decision-making has to be admitted as a premise for any contractual theory between different groups. Big firms, like big states, are here to stay. Nonetheless, the principle of pre-agreement on the main strategy to be adopted for the economy has become imperative as a condition for a working relationship between government and the unions. It is mainly the unions themselves which have proved this, through their rejection of statutory pay controls by either Conservative or Labour governments. The centralisation of economic power in the meso-economic league also has made possible the negotiation of leading companies' strategies at the national level, jointly with management and the government. Such a pre-agreement within leading companies can and should accompany joint TUC-government negotiation of the overall economic and social strategy for the nation as a whole.[40]

Rousseau's concern that political alienation should be avoided in his society has a socialist equivalent in industrial society in the concern to ensure that income is not alienated from those who earn it by a now largely functionless class of personal shareholders. The Rousseauite contract was concerned in detail with the specific means whereby such political alienation could be avoided through pre-agreement on the particular way in which society would be organised. Similarly, any social contract worth the name between organised labour and a Labour government would involve the manner in which a major redistribution of wealth in society would be achieved as a precondition for greater social justice.

One of the obvious attractions to government of the contemporary application of the concept of a social contract lies in its potential in securing a voluntary agreement from organised labour in restraining the rate of increase of wages. This would be a main feature of labour's part in the contract itself. On the other hand, there are obvious dangers for the working class if a Labour government shelters temporarily under the umbrella of such an agreement and postpones the fundamental economic and social transformation of the economy which alone would justify labour's agreement to voluntary wage restraint. Put simply, *the social contract must be a contract for trans-socialist formation on the lines of Labour's Programme 1973 and the two 1974 manifestoes.* Otherwise, organised labour would simply be contracting itself to capitalism under a Labour government. That capitalism would still be rent by such problems as high unemployment, regional imbalance, inflation, the erosion of national sovereignty by multinational capital, and so on. Under such strain, the mis-applied contract would break down, discrediting its real potential, and opening the Pandora's box of attempted statutory controls on wages.

The strategy for socialist transformation outlined in the 1973 Labour Party Programme would mean a large scale redistribution of wealth, and a wealth tax which *inter alia* reduced the compensation cost to the public from a major extension of public ownership. It also would mean the extension of such ownership beyond the infrastructure of the economy such as land and ports, weak under-capitalised sectors such as shipbuilding and high risk advanced technology sectors such as aircraft. To prove effective, socialist transformation must command the strong points in the heights of the meso-economic sector which alone can contribute decisively to solving the problems in investment, employment, the regions, prices and trade. And this means not only manufacturing enterprise and parts of the construction industry, but also financial institutions and areas in the services sector.

It is perfectly arguable that such transformation cannot be achieved in a full parliamentary term, far less overnight. Genuine transformation would take a generation and still be an ongoing process with new terms of reference and new challenge. But such transformation must be decisive, and should start now.

For its part, a Labour government must realise that a working social contract, supported by the unions, will depend on economic results which can only be achieved through transformation of the economy. And this means facing the priorities for strategic change in the new commanding heights of the meso-economic sector. Such a government would realise that socialism is not defined by whatever a Labour cabinet does. It would recognise that tactics and inspired pragmatism can only serve real change if undertaken in the framework of a strategy for transforming capitalism. It would appreciate that while the government's job is to govern, this is a confusion of means with ends unless the government admits the scale of change necessary to deserve continuing support from the unions and the public at large.

In short, if the social contract is to work, it must be a contract for socialism. The radical policies shaped by the Party since 1970 are necessarily contentious precisely because they are radical. But this is their strength as a programme provided the government can show now that it can implement in office what was shaped in opposition. If it does not, both the social contract and the socialist challenge of which it is part may prove to have been the Party's last chance to stem a national decline threatening the framework of democratic society.

References

1.   Michael Barratt Brown, *From Labourism to Socialism*, Spokesman Books, 1972, pp. 18-19.
2.   Opposition Green Paper, *Capital and Equality*, Report of a Labour Party Study Group, 1973.
3.   A.B. Atkinson, *Unequal Shares*, Allen Lane, 1972, chapter 1.
4.   C.A.R. Crosland, *The Future of Socialism*, Jonathan Cape, 1956. Twenty years later Crosland was writing that "it is a great comfort that everyone now seems to agree that socialism is about equality". See Anthony Crosland, *Socialism Now and Other Essays*, Jonathan Cape, 1974, p. 125.
5.   Commenting on the Crosland definition of 'socialism' as willingness to give an "exceptional priority" to "overcoming poverty, distress and social squalor" Abel-Smith drily commented: "I would conclude that a man from Mars, given Crosland's definition of socialism and the official statistics, might easily make a mistake in his efforts to identify the Socialist Party." Cf. *Socialiam and Affluence*, The Fabian Society, and further Ken Coates, *The Crisis of British Socialism*, Spokesman Books, 1972.
6.   Michael Meacher, "The Coming Class Struggle", *The New Statesman*, 4 January 1974.
7.   Frank Blackaby, "The Living Standard", *New Society*, 17 October 1974. The figures are for an average male employee married with two children of 11 or under. I am grateful to Donald Roy for drawing this article to my attention.
8.   See J.M. Keynes, *The General Theory of Employment, Interest and Money*, Macmillan, 1936, p. 378.
9.   C.A.R. Crosland, *The Future of Socialism*, op. cit.
10.   Department of Economic Affairs, *The Task Ahead*, 1969.
11.   S.J. Prais, *A New Look at Industrial Concentration*, Oxford Economic Paper, July 1974.
12.   Gerald Newbould and Andrew Jackson, *The Receding Ideal*, Guthstead, 1972.
13.   Greek *macros* — large; *micros* — small; *mesos* — intermediate.
14.   Anthony Crosland, *Socialism Now*, op. cit., p. 32.
15.   Derek Channon, *The Strategy and Structure of British Enterprise*, Macmillan, 1973.
16.   The Labour Party, *The National Enterprise Board*, 1972.
17.   See further, Wayland Kennet, Larry Whitty and Stuart Holland, *Sovereignty and Multinational Companies*, Fabian Tract, 1971.
18.   Report of the Committee of Enquiry on Small Firms, *Small Firms*, Cmnd. 4811, HMSO November 1971.
19.   Aubrey Jones, *The New Inflation*, Andre Deutsch, 1973, p. 109.
20.   Michael Barratt Brown, *From Labourism to Socialism*, op. cit.
21.   Mervyn King, *The Guardian*, 14 November 1973.
22.   Richard Pryke, *Public Enterprise in Practice*, McGibbon and Kee, 1971.

23.   See Donald Roy, *State Holding Companies,* Fabian Pamphlet no.
       40, October 1974. The daily subsidy figure assumes a five day
       week for 52 weeks a year. Allowing for closure during holidays
       would give a figure nearer £10 million per working day.
24.   Geoff Wood, "Why Small Firms Lose in the Fight for Grants", *The
       Financial Times,* 8th May 1973.
25.   Second Report from the Commons Expenditure Committee,
       Regional Development Incentives, Minutes of Evidence, 1973.
26.   A typical example of such a follow-the-leader effect in electronics
       was given by ITT Semiconductor's introducing a new range of
       integrated circuit devices at the end of 1972. Motorola subsequent-
       ly announced the expansion of its competitive range. In June 1973
       Texas Instrument's announcement of an expanded range of devices
       in the TTL 74 series followed announcement the same month of
       the development of the Process III by-polar devices by Plessey.
27.   Cf. A.J. Brown, *The Framework of Regional Economics in the
       United Kingdom,* NIESR and Cambridge University Press, 1972.
28.   See further, Stuart Holland, *Multinational Companies and a Selec-
       tive Regional Policy,* Memorandum to the Commons Expenditure
       Committee 1973, reprinted in Second Report from the Expendi-
       ture Committee, *Regional Development Incentives,* Minutes of
       Evidence, January 1974.
29.   Cf. further *Multinational Companies,* etc. ibid. Reliant Motors
       was one of the medium sized firms submitting credible evidence
       on IDC difficulties.
30.   Bank of Italy, *Annual Report,* 1973.
31.   IRI, *Annual Report,* 1972.
32.   Cf. Roy Jenkins, *What Matters Now,* Fontana, 1972, chapter 2.
33.   Andrew Shonfield, *Modern Capitalism,* RIIA and Oxford University
       Press, 1965.
34.   It took the FBI's exploitation and a particularly amnesiac executive
       who had kept a notebook of bid codes, pseudonyms etc. in col-
       lusion to crack the case and bring the culprits to court. The Anti-
       Trust Division previously found that they were cracking their heads
       on a closed door. Cf. Richard Austin Smith, *Corporations in
       Crisis,* Doubleday-Anchor, 1963.
35.   In December 1973 Category 1 included 180 companies excluding
       public enterprise. This was recognised as a workable number of
       firms for direct government intervention (under the Tory
       Counter-Inflation Policy) despite the fact that the Tories are
       claiming in early 1975 that the Planning Agreements system *for
       the same firms* would be unworkable.
36.   Labour's Programme, 1973, pp. 17-18.
37.   Trades Union Congress, *Industrial Democracy,* Interim Report
       by the TUC General Council, 1973, and *Industrial Democracy,*
       Report (ibid), 1974.
38.   Tony Benn, *Speeches,* Spokesman Books, 1974.
39.   Basically, State capitalism amounts to the State intervening to
       do those jobs which private capitalism will not do. The logical
       outcome of such intervention is State intrepreneurship, or the
       State as both owner and manager of the means of production,
       distribution and exchange. It is the path of intervention in the
       structure of supply which Keynes thought would be rendered

unnecessary by demand management policies. It also is a path which has been followed some way by the Italians since the late 1950's, and with varying degrees of reluctance by governments in France, Belgium, Sweden, Canada and Australia, and many less developed countries.

40.   If there is an original written contract without the name it is the TUC-Labour Party Liaison Committee document, *Economic Policy and the Cost of Living,* February 1973, in terms of Figure 7, the on-going negotiation on the contract happens between the TUC and the Cabinet, at the top of the diagram. Individual union policy is negotiated through union structures (in the left-hand column) and joint union policy in the Planning Agreements system through the company and corporation structures (in the right-hand column).

Table 1

Numbers of companies in the 22 main industrial classifications which held 50 per cent or more of the net assets in their classifications at end-1957 and end-1967*

Classification	End-1957 number	End-1967* number
Food	7	4
Drink	12	4
Tobacco	1	1
Chemicals and allied industries	2	2
Metal manufacture	6	4
Non-electrical engineering	23	19
Electrical engineering	5	3
Shipbuilding and marine engineering	4	3
Vehicles	5	2
Metal goods n.e.s.	2	2
Textiles	8	3
Leather, leather goods and fur	3	3
Clothing and footwear	3	1
Bricks, pottery, glass, cement, etc.	6	6
Timber, furniture etc.	5	6
Paper, printing and publishing	6	3
Other manufacturing	2	1
Construction	7	5
Transport and communication (excl. shipping)	4	3
Wholesale distribution	21	14
Retail distribution	6	6
Miscellaneous services	4	5

*Adjusted for mergers which took place in 1968

Source: Dept. of Trade & Industry. *A Survey of Mergers 1958-68, 1970*

Table 2
Monopoly Power and Household Goods

Product	Number of Companies		Owning Companies
Wallpaper	2	90%	ICI and WPM
Frozen fish and veg	2	90%	Unilever and Findus (Nestlé-Lyons)
Tinned soups	3	90%	Nestlé, Heinz, Campbell's
Powdered soups	3	80%	Nestlé, Unilever, Knorr
Margarine	3	80%	Unilever, Kraft, CWS
Condensed & Evaporated Milk	3	80%	Nestle, Libby, Carnation
Instant coffee	3	95%	Nestlé, Lyons, Maxwell House (General Foods)
Detergents and soaps	2	90%	Unilever, Proctor & Gamble
Salt	2	90%	ICI, British Salt Company (Cerebos-Staveley)
Ice cream	2	85%	Unilever, Lyons
Gin	2	80%	Distillers, James Burrough
Colour film	1	90%	Kodak
Television tubes	3	80%	Thorn, Philips, GEC
Single records	3	70%	Philips, EMI, Decca

Source: G. Walshe, *Recent Trends in Monopoly in Great Britain*, National Institute of Economic and Social Research, Occasional Paper 27, 1974.

* These are the latest available estimates by the National Institute. Some of the figures date only from the later 1960's. This shows the urgent need for systematic up to date public information on big companies of the kind which will operate through Labour's Planning Agreements system.

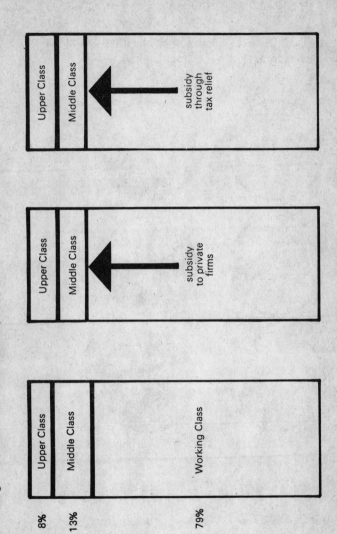

Figure 1. Class Structure and Inequality

Upper Class — 8%
Middle Class — 13%
Working Class — 79%

Upper Class
Middle Class
subsidy to private firms

Upper Class
Middle Class
subsidy through tax relief

Figure 2. How the Upper and Middle Class Own all Income from Wealth (i.e. from Capital)

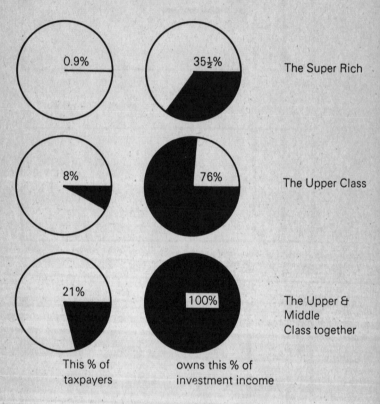

The Super Rich

The Upper Class

The Upper & Middle Class together

This % of taxpayers   owns this % of investment income

Source: The Labour Party Green Paper *Capital and Equality* 1973

Figure 3. The Trend to Monopoly in British Manufacturing

Share of top hundred companies in Manufacturing output

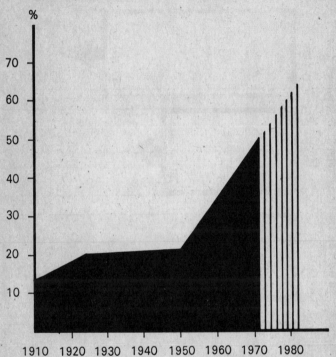

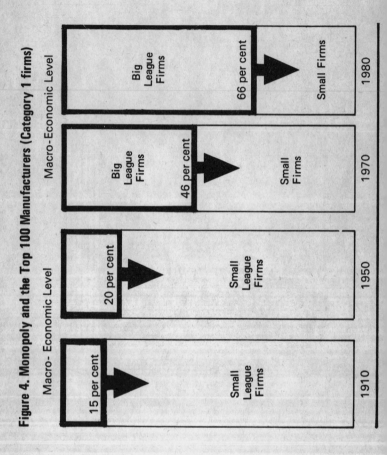

Figure 4. Monopoly and the Top 100 Manufacturers (Category 1 firms)

Figure 5. New Public Enterprise and the Planning Agreements System

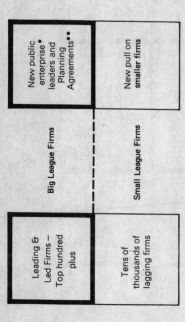

	Big League Firms	New public enterprise * leaders and Planning Agreements **
Leading & Led Firms – Top hundred plus		
Tens of thousands of lagging firms		New pull on smaller firms
	Small League Firms	

* National Enterprise Board (State Holding Company) To build up to 1 in 4 or 1 in 5 (20 to 25) of top hundred over a parliamentary term (opposition Green Paper 1972)

** Planning Agreements – advance scrutiny of leading 100 to 180 companies including public corporations with public money only granted for revealed need in return for right to take a public shareholding.

Note

Both the National Enterprise Board and the Planning Agreements system should be used to promote the main aims of social and economic policy including (Labour's Programme 1973 p. 33):-

1. Job creation, especially in areas of high unemployment;
2. Investment Promotion and newly embodied technology, raising output per worker;
3. Raising Exports and Reducing Import Costs and Volume;
4. Tackling the spread of multinational companies;
5. Restraining price increases (partly through reducing the inflation effect in transfer pricing
6. The Spread of Industrial Democracy.

Figure 6. Workers' Control and Joint Workers' Negotiation of Planning Agreements

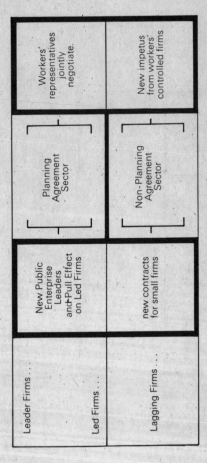

	Planning Agreement Sector	Non-Planning Agreement Sector
Leader Firms . . .	New Public Enterprise Leaders and Pull Effect on Led Firms	Workers' representatives jointly negotiate.
Led Firms . . .		
Lagging Firms . . .	new contracts for small firms	New impetus from workers' controlled firms

Note

Constituent firms in the Planning Agreements Sector (up to 180 top firms and public corporations) can be worker controlled without conflict with the public interest through the bargaining out of Planning Agreements.

Worker controlled firms outside the Planning Agreements system are small enough not to directly affect the public interest on jobs, trade etc on a major scale.

In general the Planning Agreements system will serve to *promote* the public interest through increasing jobs, trade, investment etc., while restraining inflation, on the lines in Labour's Programme 1973 and diagram

Figure 7. Framework for Bargaining of Planning Agreements and the Social Contract

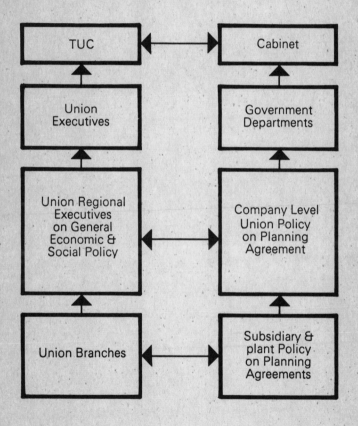